INSIDE THE WOMB, A BABY ALREADY KNOWS HOW TO . . .

- Manage his mother's body, altering its shape, behavior—and even its preferences for foods that are more beneficial to *his* growth .... **at *1–2 months gestation***

- Transform herself from a cluster of cells to a miniature human of recognizable gender .... **at *3 months gestation***

- Dream during sleep, thus stimulating the budding brain .... **at *5 months gestation***

- Mimic the action of breathing, inhaling, and exhaling amniotic fluid, thus preparing herself for the moment of birth .... **at *6 months gestation***

- Sense his mother's mood just by listening to the tone of her voice—and react to it .... **at *7 months gestation***

- Send his mother the complex chemical message that triggers her first contraction .... **at *9 months gestation***

HOW LIFE BEGINS
The Science of Life in the Womb

❦

"A FASCINATING BOOK . . . FILLED WITH TIDBITS THAT WILL SHOCK AND DELIGHT."

—*Santa Cruz Sentinel*

QUANTITY SALES

Most Dell books are available at special quantity discounts when purchased in bulk by corporations, organizations, or groups. Special imprints, messages, and excerpts can be produced to meet your needs. For more information, write to: Dell Publishing, 1540 Broadway, New York, NY 10036. Attention: Special Markets.

INDIVIDUAL SALES

Are there any Dell books you want but cannot find in your local stores? If so, you can order them directly from us. You can get any Dell book currently in print. For a complete up-to-date listing of our books and information on how to order, write to: Dell Readers Service, Box DR, 1540 Broadway, New York, NY 10036.

HOW LIFE BEGINS

The Science of Life in the Womb

CHRISTOPHER VAUGHAN

Illustrations: Marni Fylling

A Dell Trade Paperback

A DELL TRADE PAPERBACK

Published by
Dell Publishing
a division of
Bantam Doubleday Dell Publishing Group, Inc.
1540 Broadway
New York, New York 10036

If you purchased this book without a cover you should be aware that this book
is stolen property. It was reported as "unsold and destroyed" to the publisher
and neither the author nor the publisher has received any payment for this
"stripped book."

Copyright © 1996 by Christopher Vaughan

Illustrations copyright © 1996 by Marni Fylling

All rights reserved. No part of this book may be reproduced or transmitted in
any form or by any means, electronic or mechanical, including photocopying,
recording, or by any information storage and retrieval system, without the
written permission of the Publisher, except where permitted by law. For
information address: Times Books, a division of Random House, Inc., New
York, New York.

The trademark Dell® is registered in the U.S. Patent and Trademark Office.

ISBN: 0-440-50800-2

Reprinted by arrangement with Times Books

Printed in the United States of America

Published simultaneously in Canada

September 1997

10 9 8 7 6 5 4 3 2 1

BVG

CG
525
V38
1997

To Laurie, with love,
For all you've brought me

Acknowledgments

Thanks go to my agent, Gail Ross, who assisted in this book's conception and naming, and to my editor at Times Books, Betsy Rapoport, who helped develop and deliver something more beautiful than I ever could have produced on my own. To Marni Fylling, for creating elegant illustrations on short notice. To the many physicians and scientists, named and unnamed, who work long hours to do such incredible research while running laboratories and scrambling for tight funds. Many of them gave a great deal

of their valuable time to me, which I very much appreci-
ate. Lastly, thanks go to my family, for liking what I did,
and especially to my wife (always my best editor) for both
liking what I did and telling me exactly what she didn't
like and why. She deserves extra praise for her research efforts: during her pregnancies she faithfully described to
me every feeling of sickness and discomfort, every moment of wonder and joy.

Foreword

This book was born of two parents: personal curiosity and
professional interest. When my wife, Laurie, and I began
talking about having children I wanted to know all I could
about a child's growing and becoming inside the womb.
The existing pregnancy books were interesting but not
fully satisfying, because they mostly focused on how pregnancy progressed for the mother and didn't flesh out the
details of how a single cell becomes a self, how life progressed in the womb. I found myself turning to medical

textbooks and medical journals. But the information there was couched in arcane terminology and tended to have an understandable but gruesome focus on what can go wrong rather than what happens when things go right.

My interest was also spurred as a result of my work as a journalist, writing news stories for magazines like *Science News* and the British magazine *New Scientist*. Every week seemed to bring a new story about the ongoing revolution in the science of embryonic and fetal development, a new discovery about the how and why of morning sickness or the chemistry of labor. New fertility techniques have brought a greater understanding of how healthy pregnancies can be promoted. New genetic and analytical techniques have allowed researchers to plumb the details of how the body is built from so little. And new scanning technologies such as ultrasound and magnetic resonance have offered scientists a new window into the womb, and have given them a new appreciation for the rich life and behavior of the fetus in the womb.

This book is an attempt to illuminate the wonders of normal human development for a broader public that may not have any scientific or medical training. It is a survey of the most fascinating aspects of the first nine months of the fetus' life, an album of life inside the womb.

The following chapters cover how the baby-to-be stage-manages a mother's body, altering her behavior and body shape, as well as initiating the first contractions in labor. They look at the new understanding of how genes mold the mind and body. They describe how babies in the womb appear to be dreaming, and how this may be critical for brain development. In the effort to portray the whole of what we know about life's origins, the book reaches back far into the past to explore why sex became part of reproduction. It also looks forward to explain why many of the basic processes of prenatal development don't stop at birth. In fact, they remain active throughout our lives; even our ability to learn and change is dependent on those processes.

Strangely enough, the development of the book followed the pattern of Laurie's first pregnancy. I even signed the contract the same week my son, Adam, was conceived. Although writing the book took much longer than the pregnancy, it also seemed to break down into familiar trimesters. The first trimester I was excited but a little nervous and queasy about such a gargantuan task. The second trimester I was feeling good, and the writing was really rolling along as the book grew. In the third trimester the weight of it was on me night and day. I couldn't sleep. People asked if I was *still* writing that book. Then my due date came and went and still no book. I just wanted it over.

Now that Adam is born and the book is finished, I am more awed than ever by what I've learned about development, both from my research and from watching him grow. I hope I can share a little bit of that awe in this scientific voyage back to the place we've all been but have all forgotten, this little peek at the hidden world of life in the womb.

September 1995

Contents

HOW LIFE BEGINS

PROLOGUE

BIRTH

The history of man for the nine months
preceding his birth would probably be
far more interesting, and contain events
of greater moment, than all the three
score and ten years that follow it.
—*Samuel Taylor Coleridge*

SIXTEEN YEARS BEFORE HE GETS HIS DRIVER'S LICENSE, THE little boy is taking his mother for a ride. He drives her back and forth, up and down the blue industrial carpet outside the birthing room. He pushes her along in an awkward waddle until the brakes are applied—wham!—every five minutes as the band of muscles around her belly clenches, forcing her to halt and catch her breath. A nervous and concerned father is in tow. Both parents know there is no getting off and no turning back. It's shaping up to be a wild and scary yet exhilarating trip, as joyrides often are.

For thirty-eight weeks the boy has been content to drift, kick, and paddle inside his mother's womb, sucking up nutrition through his umbilical straw and pushing blood back through to pick up more groceries in the placenta. He has been inhaling and exhaling the warm, salty amniotic fluid that surrounds him and also gulping it down, tasting and smelling it. He has been listening to muffled conversations from the outer world and hearing the musical counterpoint of his mother's heart, lungs, stomach, and intestines. With gradually opening eyes and curled hands, he has investigated the limits of his cramped, twilight world.

In the last few weeks before birth, the boy has experienced a crescendo of brain activity. The flashes of nerve pulses in disparate networks have begun to coalesce. The chemical and electrical signals passing through his tiny body have started to connect, to gather together. Like delegates at a grand convention, his lungs, his heart, his hormonal system, and a thousand other circuits have come together under one banner, voting in a single proclamation: It is time to be born. For it is the baby who decides when the time is ripe, he who starts up the engines of birth.

Nerve centers deep in the fetal brain have been monitoring the development of these vital organs and systems. When all sectors show themselves prepared, the baby's body signals that it is ready (and some unknown signal from the mother agrees) with a chemical whisper from part of a pea-sized section of the brain called the hypothalamus. The recipient of this "go" signal, the pituitary gland, amplifies it by spurting a chemical called ACTH into the baby's bloodstream, which travels through the blood to the minute adrenal glands perched atop his kidneys. There, the ACTH mobilizes an even larger spurt of a stress hormone, cortisol. Now the engines are revved; it's time to engage the gears.

Throughout pregnancy, a particular ratio of the hormones estrogen and progesterone has kept the mother's abdominal muscles in a wobbly equilibrium: muscles tense and relax in very slight contractions that are suppressed before they become too strong. Now, the baby's production of estrogen shifts the balance of estrogen and progesterone, causing a chain reaction of biochemical events. Thereafter, contractions are promoted, and the tightening of muscles intensifies as labor begins.

Now that the baby has made the decision to be born, his mother probably feels as she did the first time she rode a roller coaster and the cars ratcheted up the first hill—part of her wants to go back, but she knows she's got to hold on and wait for her stomach to drop. Ahead lie hours of hard labor, when her child will take her to another world, bringing her the closest she may ever be to her own animality. When it is nearly over, the push through the birth canal will squeeze the amniotic fluid from the boy's lungs; his head will make many attempts at breaching the wall to the world outside, and finally succeed. The cold and dry air on his face will startle him into drawing the first of millions of breaths that follow.

While the moment of birth is the beginning of many stories, it is also the end of a huge and neglected chapter in our existence. Neglected mostly because the world of the womb has been hidden to those outside it. Knowing so little about what is going on in the fetus's chamber, we cannot fathom the miracles taking place there.

Life in the womb is a journey we have all taken but forgotten, a period that links our present to the whole history of life on earth, a time that shapes our lives and perceptions into adulthood. In the last decade or two, scientists have begun to widen our perspective on the course of that journey. This book attempts to gather insights from the most exciting basic and clinical research on development and use them to illuminate life in the womb. It focuses on the experiences of the embryo and fetus and tries to provide an easily understandable picture of the long and fascinating journey from single cell to plump and bright-eyed baby.

A NOTE ON TIMING

TRYING TO FIGURE YOUR BABY'S DUE DATE OR IMAGINE what's going on during pregnancy at any given time can be very frustrating. This is partly because there are four ways to measure the duration of pregnancy: in calendar months (which vary in length), in lunar months (four weeks), in weeks, or in days. The confusion is compounded by the system obstetricians use. Because women's ovulation cycles vary, doctors don't know exactly when fertilization took place. So they find out the date of the beginning of the last menstrual period (LMP) and count that as day zero, or the moment of conception, designating the baby's due date a neat ten lunar months (forty weeks) later.

The problem with this system is that since most women ovulate, or produce an egg, fourteen days (two weeks) after their LMP, the embryo is "two weeks old" at the moment of actual conception, and the stated age of the embryo continues to be two weeks off for the rest of the pregnancy. In other words, most obstetricians figures are based on a forty-week pregnancy when you're actually pregnant for only thirty-eight weeks.

The frustration results partly because books on pregnancy usually don't say whether they are using calendar months or lunar months—or whether they are counting weeks since conception or weeks after the last menstrual period—when they are describing what is happening during pregnancy. Knowing which system your obstetrician uses and how old your baby really is—how long since the actual moment of conception—is especially important in the early months, when things are changing on a daily basis.

This book marks the weeks in the baby's "true" age, or calendar age, the age from actual conception. This differs from the system used by most obstetricians and most pregnancy books. But the true age is more straightforward and less confusing for people trying to find out what events are taking place when. The other reason I've used this system is that many women now know, through temperature readings or ovulation predictor kits, exactly when they ovulate. They often know exactly when conception must have taken place and therefore know the baby's true age.*

In addition, most people don't measure time in lunar months, and trying to make a quick measure of what lunar month you are in requires constant consultation with a calendar and a lot of page flipping. For this reason, in this book I have tried to approximate calendar months as closely as possible, so that if conception occurred on the 27th of one month, the new month would begin on the 27th of the next. This method uses four-week periods for each month and adds a week every few months to bring the two systems back in line with each other.

---

*Most doctors dismiss as conjecture any talk about probable dates of conception. They prefer instead to calculate from the date of the last menstrual period because that method deals only with "known facts' and seems more "scientific." But if doctors counted forward fourteen days from the LMP and used that date as day zero, they would be no more or less accurate or "scientific," and that date would be closer to the day of conception, resulting in a closer estimate of the baby's true age.

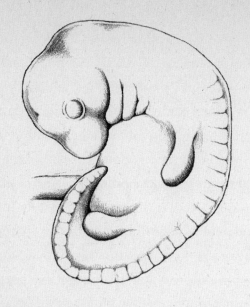

actual size

THE FIRST MONTH

(Weeks 1–4 after conception;
weeks 3–6 after LMP)

The first month following conception—the union of sperm and egg—is a period of tremendous activity for the developing embryo. Yet from a developmental perspective, the first four weeks could almost be divided in half—two weeks when nothing seems to happen, followed by two weeks in which everything seems to happen with astonishing speed. During the first two weeks, there is little that is even recognizable as the embryo. Though a lot is going on on a cellular level, the embryo and its surrounding tissue (sometimes called the preembryo) look like nothing but a clump of undifferentiated cells. In the second two weeks, however, the embryo becomes clearly separate and identifiable, and limbs and major organs form.

During the first week after conception, the fertilized egg cell begins to divide exponentially, splitting into two cells, then four, eight, sixteen, and so on. By the end of the first week, it has become a hollow ball of a few hundred cells, with a swelled mass of cells on one side, a mass which will become the embryo and fetus.

It is at this stage or slightly earlier that identical (or monozygotic) twins are created. In about one-quarter of one percent of all births, the whole ball of cells or the inner cells mass splits apart and creates two embryos. The reasons for this are unknown. What is known is that the birth rate of identical twins remains the same for all ethnic groups around the world. Fraternal (or dizygotic) twins, on the other hand, tend to be more common in some groups and families. Fraternal twins are created when two eggs are released at the same time and both are fertilized and implanted in the womb.

During the fifth or sixth day of this first week, the embryo implants itself into the uterine wall. Until this time, the ball of cells hasn't grown in size at all; even though it has divided many times, it has split the material it has, each cell doling out its inheritance among its progeny. As a result, the preembryo has remained no thicker than a piece of typing paper—about .14 millimeters.

During the second week, the tissue that will become the placenta begins establishing a link with the mother's blood supply. Once the link is established, the embryo will finally be able to pick up more building materials and grow larger. Until then, it remains a flat disc of cells sandwiched between two fluid-filled sacs in a ball (the yolk sac and the smaller amniotic sac; see Chapter 3). During this time, the yolk sac starts making blood. It will serve as the baby's factory for blood cells until the liver, spleen, and then bone marrow can take over the job.

During these first two weeks, many women don't even know that they are pregnant. Fortunately, there is no evidence that anything they eat, drink, or do during the first two weeks will cause birth defects. Any changes in development during the first fourteen days will be either so major that they will end the pregnancy or so minor that they will be ignored and corrected. Amazingly, even the death of one cell at the four-cell stage—the removal of one-quarter of the preembryo—will not halt or alter a normal pregnancy.

In the third week (the fifth week from LMP), the embryonic disc begins to fold itself by changing the shape of individual cells and making some multiply faster than others. The tubular structure of the embryo's body forms, and the long slit of the neural groove opens, where the spinal cord will develop. One end of this groove begins to bend where the brain will form. Small, paired clumps of cells begin to gather on either side of the groove where vertebrae and muscles will later appear. A lump appears where the heart tube is beginning to form, and blood vessels begin to link up. At the end of the third week, the embryo is 1.5–2.0 millimeters long, about the thickness of two dimes.

During the fourth week (sixth week after LMP), things really begin to come together. The two tubes of the heart fuse and start contracting by the 22nd day (the first day of the fourth week). At first the heart simply pushes blood back and forth through the body, but by the 25th day it is beating properly, moving blood in one direction. At this point, blood circulates between the embryo, the yolk sac, and through the newly created umbilical cord. The neural tube zips itself shut during week four. It is during this time that one of the B vitamins can help babies avoid spina bifida, a birth defect that results when the spinal cord doesn't close completely.

The fourth week is also when the embryo's sex cells migrate to the proper location. These germ cells, the cells that are destined to become sperm or egg and produce future generations, start out in the yolk sac. During the fourth week they move to the gonadal ridge, where the testes or ovaries will later form around them.

The folds of the head and face become distinct during this week, and there are spots where the eyes and the ears are beginning to form. Tiny bumps are rising where the arms and legs will appear. The beginnings of the thyroid gland, lungs, liver, pancreas, and kidneys are all identifiable. By the end of the month, the embryo is curled into an arc 4 millimeters across (about the size of a small pea).

ONE

SEX AND THE

SINGLE CELL

WHAT IS SEX? AND WHAT'S THE POINT OF IT? ALTHOUGH these might seem to be pretty rudimentary questions, they have long been the object of intense study. And we still don't know the full answers. Perhaps the first real steps toward an answer were taken over three hundred years ago in Europe.

Animalcules

In October 1677, as autumnal winds began to cool the fields and canals around Delft, in the Netherlands, a medical student brought Antonie van Leeuwenhoek (lay-ven-hook) an interesting sample: semen from a patient bothered by venereal disease. Although Leeuwenhoek sold draperies and cloth, he didn't find it strange that someone would bring him such an offering. After all, Leeuwenhoek was known in scientific circles as a wizard at making and using the newly invented microscope. While other European scientists were studying the microscopic structures in insects and plants, Leeuwenhoek was inspecting lowly specimens such as pond scum and stagnant water. There he found a whole world of tiny eel-like creatures and living blobs. He called these "animalcules."

Leeuwenhoek had always resisted looking at semen under the microscope because it seemed immodest, even profane, in the strongly religious milieu of time. And yet, if it was a medical problem . . . perhaps the microscope could cast some light on the subject.

Leeuwenhoek peered at the sample through one of his microscopes and was amazed to find uncountable multitudes of little animals, each with a bulbous head less than a millionth the size of a grain of sand and a long, undulating tail. Could this be in all semen, or was it part of the disease? Or perhaps these animalcules had grown since the sample had been taken, just as creatures seemed to grow in water he let stand for a week.

Always one for immaculate scientific technique, Leeuwenhoek proceeded to acquire some of his own semen for comparison. He made sure not to collect the sample through sinful self-abuse, but rather during the act of making love to his wife. In order to obtain the freshest possible sample, Leeuwenhoek reported in a letter to the Royal Society in England, he jumped up, collected the specimen, popped it into the microscope, and inspected it "immediately after ejaculation, before six heartbeats had passed." There he saw the same animalcules.

We can only imagine what Leeuwenhoek's wife thought of her place in history.

Leeuwenhoek's letter ignited a centuries-long argument about whether the sperm or the egg was the source of the human fetus. Leeuwenhoek believed that sperm were merely parasitic animals living in the semen, while others believed that all the components of a human were already contained in the sperm. All that was needed, they said, was to plant the sperm in the fertile matrix of the womb. One contemporary thought a tiny, preformed baby lay balled in the fetal position inside each sperm. An opposing camp felt that the egg was the seed of life, awaiting only the animating "life-force" contained in the male semen. The argument was not resolved for nearly 250 years.

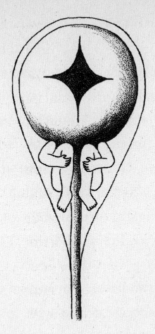

Copy of a seventeenth-century drawing showing one idea of how babies originated in sperm.

Today these ideas seem simpleminded. We know, of course, that neither sperm nor egg alone contains all the ingredients of life. They must combine forces to make a new life. And we know that there is no microscopic baby, with little hands and toes, waiting inside either the sperm or egg.

Although most adults believe they know all the "facts of life," scientists are finding that we really know very little about exactly what goes on during fertilization. Evidence of this is the fact that at least 15 percent of all cases of infertility are of unexplained origin, meaning we don't know what's going wrong because we don't know where to look for the problem. Theoretically, in vitro fertilization, in which sperm and egg are mixed outside the body before implantation in the womb, should be a simple solution for infertile couples. But it's not. In vitro fertilization fails 80 percent of the time. Our modern, can-do culture is humbled to find that flying the space shuttle will never be like taking the family station wagon on a weekend drive and that making embryos in the laboratory is not as simple as baking a cake.

There is hope, however, that current research will better the odds. Scientists, armed with recently developed tools of modern biology, are learning a great deal about the process of fertilization. Some of the new information is quite surprising. For instance, some researchers now theorize that the use of sex for reproduction—as opposed to, say, simply splitting our cells to produce carbon copies of ourselves—may be completely the result of historical accident. A fossil. Kind of like the appendix, but a lot more fun. To understand how this can be, and how we ever rose out of the primordial muck in the first place, we need to study the history of sex.

When life first began to appear in the form of single-celled creatures about 3.5 billion years ago, Earth was a tough neighborhood. The planet had formed only a billion years before, and protective gases such as ozone, which block out dangerous ultraviolet (UV) rays, were not yet in plentiful supply. UV rays are harmful because they tend to smash apart deoxyribonucleic acid (DNA), the molecule that carries the genetic code so crucial for life's existence. When cells were bombarded by so much UV radiation, their lives were put in constant jeopardy.

One leading theory is that sex, albeit a primitive, boring sort of sex, began as a way for cells to defend themselves against the UV rays. Cells may have huddled next to each other and exchanged bits of DNA, like neighbors trading flour and sugar across the back fence. If one cell's DNA was damaged, it was able to survive by getting "good" DNA from a healthy acquaintance.

A competing theory is that DNA itself initiated sex. The idea is that a particular bit of DNA developed accidentally and carried the instructions that made one cell pass it along to another. This "selfish" DNA would then propagate itself among most of the cells by making such "matings" (DNA transfers) commonplace.

But these modes of intercourse between organisms seem more social than sexual. Sex still had nothing to do with reproduction. Instead, cells were stuck in the dead-end job of reproducing by cell division. Each cell would simply fission into identical clones and separate.

Life might have stayed in such a lowly and boring state had not cells got the urge to merge, to fuse together and become one. Cell mergers may have first taken place among unrelated cell types. Some cells probably swallowed a smaller neighbor and, rather than digesting it, kept it captive in a mutually beneficial, symbiotic relationship. Scientists can still see these captives today: every cell in our bodies is actually composed of many organelles, distinct structures whose ancestors were once free-living organisms. For example, the mitochondrion, the cell's "powerhouse," still has its own DNA, and the whiplike tail of the sperm may be the descendant of a bacterial spirochete that insinuated itself into a cell.

Merging may help cells survive on limited resources, like businesses consolidating to survive hard times. Three billion years ago, cells may have merged when faced with shortages, divided in boom times, and merged again during the next bust.

Sex and reproduction were linked when two cells not only merged but also traded genes by exchanging bits of DNA. A newly merged cell had two complete sets of genes encoded in its DNA, one from each parent cell. The cell exchanged genes in the two sets of DNA, like kids shuffling two sets of baseball cards and sorting them back into two distinct piles. After shuffling its two sets of DNA, a cell would split again, creating two new cells, each with a different combination of genes.

Shuffling genes is beneficial to species. To use the baseball card example, the odds are that, after shuffling, one kid will end up with more of the "good" cards than the other. When the cell splits into two new cells after shuffling genes, one cell can be better than either of the two that entered into the shuffling process. This improved cell will be more likely than other cells to survive, lending an evolutionary benefit to sex.

But is sexual reproduction still beneficial for higher organisms, like us? Sure, sex is great fun, and comedians would have little to joke about without it, but isn't sex really a big waste of time? Scientists have been seriously pondering this question for some years. After all, in any sexual species, a tremendous amount of time and energy is spent in courting, and sexual display can often be awkward and actually make an individual less fit in a survival situation. Good examples of this are the unwieldy feather display of the peacock, the heavy, branched horns of the elk, and the stiletto heels worn by female *Homo sapiens.* Why don't we drop the dating, the muscle cars, and the string bikinis, and just reproduce by cloning ourselves?

There are two likely answers. One is that, on balance, sex is beneficial in the long run. When genes are shuffled, diversity results—and there is a likelihood that at least one combination of genes will be "best" for changing environmental conditions.

The second answer is that sex is nearly impossible to

give up. The mechanisms of sex and reproduction are so interwoven that most species are unable to separate them. In most cases, when sex is lost, reproduction is lost. Very few animals have learned how to get along without sex. Some species of lizards and salamanders have no males— the females reproduce by cloning. Some plants can switch between sexual and asexual reproduction depending on their needs. For most higher animals, including humans, such a state of affairs (or lack of affairs) seems impossible. But how did we rise from the slime, from existence as single cells, to our multicellular splendor?

The benefits of gene shuffling don't fully explain how cells moved beyond the single-cell state. How did cells change from independent creatures into the highly organized groups that make up our bodies? Perhaps it is not surprising to learn that the drive to survive and the urge to reproduce may also have been the original alchemists of this change.

One prime minister of a budding democracy once said that in her country there were five million generals. Leaders of many other democracies have felt similarly exasperated with the independence of their people. In the early days of life on Earth, cell cooperation probably had this quality of joint anarchy—each cell acted only for itself, but nevertheless they tended to group together because clustering with like cells helped each cell survive. Cells probably released digestive enzymes into the fluid around them to break down food into edible bites. Many of these cells together, therefore, could create a higher concentration of enzymes than could individual cells, making feeding easier. Groups of cells acted, in the words of one scientist, like "packs of wolves" to bring down larger prey.

But these "wolf packs" were not multicellular organisms. The cells hung out together, but didn't do much differently than they had on their own. Hunger probably changed that. To learn how this may have occurred, scientists look at curious creatures—the slime molds that inhabit Earth today.

Slime mold cells are single-celled organisms that normally live in loose cooperation in the soil. But when food is scarce, they band together and move as one organism. Cells move toward the center of the group, pushing up a mound of cells that becomes a stalk. This stalk rises up through the surface of the soil and releases spores to the wind, spreading slime mold cells to places where food might be more abundant. The cells, threatened with starvation, suddenly act cooperatively to reproduce and ensure the continuation of the species. Scientists think that this sort of action probably arose many different times in evolution.

Creatures such as the slime mold, which may be thought of as being halfway between a single-celled organism and multicellularity, never achieved much complexity because even though the cells act in concert to reproduce, they usually live in communal anarchy. But what happens if only one cell in the group retains the right to reproduce? That cell then becomes akin to a king surrounded by an army of eunuch slaves. If the king produces lots of offspring, he can turn most of them into more eunuchs to take care of his country's work. All the king needs to do to make sure this system stays in place is to create one son who can also reproduce and continue the dynasty. This kind of situation exists in beehives, where one reproducing queen is surrounded by sterile drones (and male workers, who are needed for the actual mating). If two queens are created in a hive, one is either killed or forced to leave to start a new hive.

We, and other multicellular animals, are like hives of cells. In every animal, a few basic cells retain the ability to reproduce and create billions more cells to be their eunuch army, their sterile drones. The drones can specialize so that they gather food better for the sexually reproducing cells, protecting these sex cells against the environment and making it easier for the sex cells to find and merge with their own kind. Ultimately, after performing their duties, these slave cells will fade away.

In a sense, all the non-sex cells—the cells of the muscles that pull the mouth into an alluring smile, the brain cells that take it all in and respond by signaling sexual attraction—all these cells are made to nurse the sex cells. We as organisms are collections of cells designed to surround and protect the sperm or egg cells and introduce them to their opposites. The sophisticated abilities and impressive specialties of the non-sex cells are really newfangled additions to an organism, meant to assist the ancient and primitive line of sex cells. Sperm and egg cells are the living fossils inside us.

Conceptual Drama

So when 250 million sperm (about the same number as there are people in the United States) blast into the female genital tract at the rate of 200 inches per second (10 miles an hour), they begin an ancient journey like that of some aboriginal tribe wandering across the tundra. The attrition rate of this march is enormous: so many frail, crippled, and simply lost sperm drop away that most often only a few dozen ever reach the egg.

The sperm have one mission: to find the egg and penetrate it. To make their way to the egg, they have become specialized biological machines. Over weeks in the testes, a sperm hones itself into a lean racing vehicle ready to dash for the prize at the finish line. The body of the sperm cell shrinks until it holds almost nothing but the DNA-

carrying nucleus. Even the energy-producing mitochondria are pushed out and forced to cling to the base of the
tail, the most prominent feature of the beast. The tail, or
flagellum, is a strong whip, five times the length of the
sperm body. It will push the sperm along, not by undulating back and forth as it seems to do under the microscope,
but by twirling rapidly like a corkscrew.

The womb doesn't exactly welcome the sperm—it's
an acidic environment, and the sperm must navigate a difficult course to get to the egg. During most of the woman's
monthly cycle, the pathway to the womb is blocked by
heavy mucus. This lack of hospitality is not intended as
a contraceptive, but as a safety measure. If sperm could
enter without a fight, so could infectious organisms. During ovulation, though, the mucus wall comes tumbling
down. Estrogen shapes the mucus into fernlike fronds,
allowing the sperm to scurry through like animals in heavy
underbrush.

Sperm have not one but three different kinds of swimming motions. To make the journey to the egg, each sperm
must swim a medley of all three types of motion. To wriggle through the mucus barrier, sperm straighten their tails
and lash with just the tips, as if they were equipped with
propeller shaft and propeller. The selection process begins
right away. Only sperm with good head shape and good tail
motion ever squeeze through the first slimy checkpoint.

After making their way through the mucus, sperm don't necessarily just spew into the wide open spaces of the uterus itself. The passageways in the mucus barrier lead them to holding pens. There, perhaps stilled by signals the woman's body sends, the horde of sperm can lie quietly for four to six days before coming forth. These staging areas may be responsible for pregnancies that occur when insemination takes place days before ovulation.

How do the sperm know when it's time to reactivate and venture out in search of the egg? The answer may support a view that is gaining ground with many scientists—a vision of fertilization as a collaborative act, a joint venture between sperm and egg. For a long time it has been obvious that sperm actively try to find and penetrate the egg, but until recently the egg seemed to wait passively as it floated down the fallopian tubes. Scientists have now found that the egg releases a chemical beacon, a kind of "come-hither" scent. This perfume creates a frenzy of activity among sperm and draws them toward the egg.

To some researchers, the metaphor that these signals act as some kind of scent seems particularly apt. A group of scientists in Belgium has found that sperm DNA seem to be making odor receptors. Odor receptors in the nose latch on to molecules that drift into the nostrils and allow us to detect smells. The same type of receptors may allow sperm to "follow their noses" to the egg. In fact, odor receptors may have originated as navigation aids for sperm and other single-celled organisms, and their use for detecting what we would consider smells may have come later in animal evolution.

Conceptual Drama, Scene II

When at last the sperm draw near the egg, their swimming motion changes for the last time. Now the sperm begin to thrash and flop like fish out of water. This motion may increase the chance that the sperm head will come into contact with the egg's surface. And the egg needs every chance for a sperm to bump into it, because the number of sperm that have made it this far are relatively few. The vast, teeming mass of life that was deposited at the mouth of the cervix has shrunk to a minuscule school of sperm by the time they reach the estuary of the fallopian tubes. Why is the attrition rate so great?

Part of the reason is the mucus barrier. Even when the "fronds" form, many sperm can't wriggle through. Other sperm swim blindly into the folds of the womb and get lost there. But the overriding fact is that many of the sperm are deformed, incompetent swimmers, or otherwise flawed. Only about 50 percent of all sperm produced seem to be the kind of straight-swimming, good-looking sperm that make the grade. Why so many bad apples in the barrel? The classic explanation might be termed "the inept manufacturer's excuse." This is the idea that, with 300 million sperm produced each day—hey, you're going to get some bad ones. But the body also produces millions of red blood cells every day without anything near the error rate for sperm. So the question remains.

Two British scientists have come up with an intriguing idea that the bad sperm are no accident—they are planned.

Why should bad sperm be beneficial? Robin R. Baker and Mark A. Bellis of the University of Manchester in England theorize that the bad sperm get tangled together in a way that helps create a roadblock for keeping other sperm out. In groups of primates and other mammals where many males mate with one female during her fertile period, sperm from different males can be in direct competition with each other to reach the egg first. Victory may go not only to the swift, but to the male that can impede the progress of the other guy's sperm by placing roadblocks of defective sperm.

One interesting corollary of this hypothesis is that sperm will face the stiffest competition in the most promiscuous animals—and that those animals will therefore produce more sperm (both good and bad types). In chimpanzees, many males will mate with a single female during her fertile period. Perhaps in an attempt to overwhelm their rivals' sperm, chimps produce billions of sperm in each ejaculation. Gorillas, whose sperm don't have to compete because one gorilla rules a harem of females, ejaculate a paltry 65 million sperm per shot, even though they are much larger animals. Humans, with their 250 million sperm per ejaculation, fall in the middle of this range, suggesting that our direct predecessors, while not as promiscuous as chimps, may still have been swingers.

Conceptual Drama, Scene III

When sperm actually touch the outer coat of the egg, the last stage of fertilization begins, although this event is the beginning of a sequence that scientists have studied most closely in recent years. There are three barriers any sperm must cross before actually fertilizing the egg. To breach the three, each sperm makes use of chemical weapons.

There is a collection of enzymes in the head of each sperm. When a sperm first enters the uterus, the cap covering the pouch holding these enzymes is chemically removed, in effect arming the cell's chemical warhead. The enzymes remain in the pouch, though, until the sperm comes in contact with the outermost layer of the egg (called the corona radiata) and the pouch becomes porous, allowing the enzymes to pour forth.

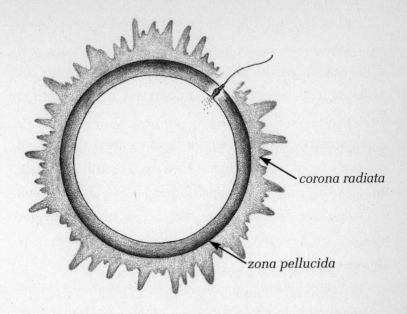

corona radiata

zona pellucida

The first obstacles to sperm offer light resistance: two layers of "cumulus" cells that surround the egg in the ovaries and cluster like faithful attendants as it journeys down the fallopian tubes.

The next layer of resistance is more difficult to breach. The zona pellucida is a relatively thick layer of protein chains with branched sugars extending from them. The zona, as it is often called, might be thought of as a ball of cotton candy around the egg. Cotton candy is a fluffy, sticky ball of spun sugar when first bought, but it turns into a dense, hard mess when it is crushed. Like cotton candy, the branched sugars of the zona pellucida weave a net around the egg cell. The zona also grabs at the sperm cells because the sperm have receptors that fit around one of the sugars on the chain. The sperm's tail spins furiously behind it as enzymes from the pouch clear a path in front of it.

By this point, many sperm have reached the egg, so this final leg of the race is hard fought. The difficult push through the zona may constitute one last test to weed out weak or defective sperm. When one sperm manages to move all the way to the egg membrane, the race is almost over.

Receptors in the sperm head bond with proteins in the egg membrane, in effect sticking a protein key into a lock. Once the two membranes are bound together, they begin to merge. Like two soap bubbles collapsing into one, the two cells' membranes fuse and the contents of the sperm gush into the interior of the egg. Instantly, chemical messengers inside the sperm spread to the egg membrane and throw open microscopic gates, allowing charged particles in the salty fluid outside the egg to rush in. This flood sends an electric jolt around the egg membrane and slams the membrane closed so no other sperm may enter. The flood of charged particles also releases a signal to the zona pellucida, and suddenly the sugary fibers bind together to form a hard shell, like crushed cotton candy.

If two sperm ever did enter the egg, there would be an

excess of genetic material in the cell. On extremely rare occasions, two sperm do enter at the same instant, but the resulting embryo soon dies.

Once inside the egg, the sperm's nucleus is pulled toward the egg's, and the two merge. In that instant, the genetic material assumes the doubled state once again and another cycle, another link, begins in the great chain of life. It is a chain of germ cells—the sperm and eggs and the cells that create them—that live two alternating existences: sometimes they live as single cells and sometimes they surround themselves with the complex structures we think of as people.

It is strange to think about, but in some ways at the moment of fertilization life doesn't so much *begin* as continue. The true beginning of human life is far at the other end of the chain, among the single cells teeming in the early seas of the planet. And so the fertilized egg seems to return to that past for a moment as it floats down the fallopian tubes in waters dark and salty, like those ancient, primordial seas.

Doctorly Husbandry

That is how fertilization is supposed to happen. And on the surface, nature seems to supply all the right ingredients to make conception easy. After all, a woman is born with about one or two million eggs. A man can pump out a thousand sperm cells per second (and produce about two trillion over the course of his life). Nature even supplies the physical apparatus for introducing the two, plus a heady blend of romance and passion powerful enough to convince even the most die-hard couch potatoes to eagerly expend the hundreds of calories the average lovemaking session consumes.

Yet often things don't work out.

Even at the best of times, when a couple makes love at the height of their fertility, during the optimal time in the woman's cycle, the chances are only one in three that a pregnancy will occur in a given month. And many couples would give anything to be blessed with such odds. In general, about one in twelve couples in the United States will experience the heartbreak of infertility, which is defined as an inability to conceive over a period of one year of sexual activity. For people in their thirties, those odds can rise to include one couple in every seven.

Infertility is not a new problem. Many wars have been fought and millions have died for lack of an heir to a throne. Historically in some cultures, it was common for a man and woman to marry only after he got her pregnant and it was obvious they could have children. What is new is the greater societal focus on infertility.

Medical researchers now believe that fertility in women decreases earlier than they previously thought. Fertility starts declining in some women as young as thirty-one years old, and the chances of having a healthy baby generally decrease 3 percent every year thereafter. By thirty-five, women need, on average, twice as many inseminations to conceive as twenty-year-old women.

What can science do to address the problem of infertility? Quite a bit can be done now that was only the stuff of science fiction forty years ago. Yet artificial fertilization is still a young science. The first "test-tube" baby, England's Louise Brown, was born in 1978, only a moment ago in the long span of medical science. Researchers have learned an amazing amount about fertilization since then. The rapidly rising success rates in artificial fertilization may be a sign that scientists in the field are entering a period wherein these lessons are rapidly turned into new techniques.

Simple artificial insemination, which counteracts a low sperm count by pooling a man's sperm and injecting it all at one time, has been used for decades. In the 1960s and 1970s, physicians learned how to manipulate elements of the menstrual cycle to increase the number of eggs released during ovulation and to make the lining of the womb more receptive to the embryo. But true in vitro fertilization (IVF) in humans began only in the late 1970s.

In in vitro (literally "in glass") fertilization, the production of eggs is artificially stimulated in a woman, and then the ripened eggs are surgically harvested with a needle. Eggs collected from this procedure are then mixed with sperm, not in a test tube but in a petri dish, a flattish, covered plate about five inches in diameter and almost always made of plastic (not glass). The fertilized egg or eggs are then implanted in the womb, with the hope that they will embed themselves in the wall of the uterus and begin a pregnancy. Problems with this method are that the woman's hormonal cycle has recently been drastically altered by the drugs that stimulate egg production, and her body may not be the most receptive it can be for the newly fertilized egg. Embryos can be frozen to give the body time to recover from this hormonal change, and some doctors feel that refinements of the freezing and thawing techniques actually lead to a higher pregnancy rate because the embryos that survive freezing are the strongest.

Advances on the basic IVF method come in the form of two techniques with the titles GIFT (gamete intrafallopian transfer) and ZIFT (zygote intrafallopian transfer). The names refer to the fact that either a zygote (the fertilized egg or embryo) or the gametes (the sperm and egg themselves) are transferred not into the womb, but into the fallopian tubes. For some unknown reason, letting the new embryo drift down the fallopian tubes into the womb, as it would naturally, dramatically increases the success rate of IVF.

The more that's learned about the process of fertilization and implantation, the more physicians will be able to find individual failures in the process and correct them specifically. The finding that eggs exude a "come-hither" perfume may allow medical researchers to isolate this factor and use it to gussy up the egg to help it attract sperm. Doctors can now test for how well sperm interact with the mucus at the beginning of their journey in the uterus, and they hope to be able to check that sperm are responding correctly to cues the whole way to the egg. For instance, for some reason a few women seem to have an immunity to their partner's sperm or the resulting embryos. These women's antibodies attack and reject the sperm or embryos as they would an invading bacterium or transplanted tissue. Finding why this is so may lead to methods of suppressing or circumventing the immune system to allow pregnancy, much as physicians do when making an organ transplant.

Scientists also have noticed that once sperm get to the egg, some have a hard time getting through the thick barriers surrounding it. In response, the scientists have found that "nicking" or poking holes in the zona pellucida helps sperm enter the egg. Some researchers are also using microscopic needles to inject a single sperm into an egg. Of course, many discoveries will be made accidentally. One such discovery is that when eggs have their zona pellucida disturbed or punctured during fertilization, they implant better in the womb than unpunctured eggs.

Perhaps one of the most significant discoveries is that women can become pregnant and bear children later than was ever thought possible. A small but growing group of women are having babies in their fifties, some after they have passed menopause. This development is based in the discovery that as women age, their eggs (present since birth) become less viable, but their reproductive plumbing can function just fine with a little maintenance. These oldest of mothers use eggs donated by younger women, and undergo hormone treatments to fire up the reproductive tract in preparation to accept the fertilized egg. There seems to be no biological reason why women cannot continue to have babies into their sixties, seventies, or later, although the physical stress of pregnancy is harder to bear for older women and complications are more common.

With such options and the promise of more advancements to come, perhaps we are coming close to true birth control—the control of reproduction.

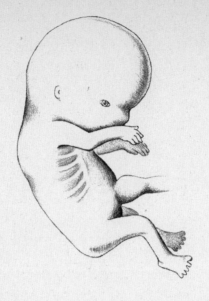

actual size

THE SECOND MONTH

(Weeks 5–8 after conception;
weeks 7–10 after LMP)

During the second month, the embryo becomes completely recognizable as a miniature human baby, and at the end of this month it is called a fetus.

In the 5th week (7th week after LMP), the embryo grows from 4 millimeters to 8 millimeters (about the size of an M&M). The arms and legs get longer and acquire slight bends where the elbows and knees will be. Tiny paddles spread at the ends of these limbs where hands and feet will develop.

The face begins to form during this week as the eyes, nose, and mouth all become identifiable—even though the profile still looks more like that of a cartoon hippo than a baby. Behind the face the basic structures of the brain are growing rapidly. At the other end of the embryo, a tail sprouts and reaches a maximum size of one tenth the length of the rest of the body. After this, the tail will shrink and the rest of the body will grow out around it until it disappears completely by birth.

In the 6th week after conception (9th week after LMP), the skeleton begins to condense out of muscle tissue. Like the first internal skeletons on earth, it is made of cartilage instead of bone. At the end of the week, bone starts laying itself down around these cartilage models. The hands and feet get rays of cartilage that will develop into fingers and toes. At this point there are no joints.

The rapidly growing liver creates a bulge in the embryo's belly next to the heart and takes over blood production from the yolk sac. At the end of the week, the embryo is about 15 millimeters long—just over half an inch and about the size of an unshelled peanut.

In the 7th and 8th weeks (9th and 10th weeks after LMP), the face develops an upper lip and nostrils set in the little nub of a nose. The neck lengthens, which makes the lower jaw stand out. The ears, which were bumpy grooves hovering around the neck during week six, have now moved to the side of the head and are surrounded by a simple flap of skin. The eyes, while still set very wide apart, move forward on the face and they become pigmented. The overshadowing forehead becomes less prominent as the baby's face grows. The mouth curves in what almost seems like a little smile.

The internal organs become well defined, the sex organs form around the germ cells, and the tail is almost completely gone. The arms, legs, fingers, and toes become thinner and more delicate. During this time, muscles in the neck and body begin to contract spontaneously, and the embryo will arch his back and push away from the edge of the amniotic sac. The movements are so small and weak, however, that they can't be felt by the mother at this time. At the end of the embryonic period is also the end of the time when most birth defects occur. At this point, the fetus is 30 millimeters (about an inch and a quarter) in length when measured from head to rump (the legs are too short to make much difference)—about the size of a two-peanut shell.

By the end of this month, the steady thump-thump-thump of the heart is often (though not always) strong enough to be heard with a "Doptone."

TWO

WHO'S WALKING WHOM?

AH, THE JOYS OF THE EXPECTANT MOTHER. SO OFTEN THE miraculous news of a new pregnancy hits like a bout of the flu. A numbing fatigue overwhelms the body. You are stricken by a cruelly paradoxical combination of gut-wrenching nausea and hunger, usually in alternation, but sometimes almost simultaneously ("I'm not hungry at all. Everything sounds so disgusting"—munch, munch—"Oh, this tastes great"). When nausea does strike, it may culminate in your first close communion with the toilet bowl since a teenage blackberry brandy bender. The violent body clench and gush of vomiting that doctors genteelly call emesis can be shocking to all concerned ("Honey, did a water pipe break in there?"). Often, women can begin to feel that they are not so much having a baby as being had by it.

In fact, the baby does practically commandeer the mother's body, and scientists have begun to discover the details of the takeover. Maternal changes in weight and diet turn out to be only part of an intricate chemical dance between mother and child. Hormones and chemical signals cross back and forth between the two, affecting embryonic growth and maternal behavior. And the embryo, in order to live within the mother, must manipulate and succor her immune system in order to override the powerful forces the body usually raises against invaders.

A great deal of this interplay between mother and child is important but hidden—it goes on without anyone noticing. Other parts, such as the physical feelings of pregnancy, are quite obvious, and people only wish they were hidden. Take heart, though: scientists are discovering that many of the difficulties of pregnancy are part of a master plan—even if nature's method drives you mad.

So Happy I Want to Throw Up

Why do so many woman, during what should be a joyful time, have to experience such nausea, aching fatigue, hunger, and vertigo? One study found that 89% of pregnant women suffer from "morning" sickness (which can last all day) and 15% of expectant mothers feel sick all the way through pregnancy. To some people it seems like a perverse payback for getting pregnant in the first place. Or perhaps it is some cosmic retribution for original sin. Scientific studies suggest a more down-to-earth cause. Although these symptoms suggest an illness, experiment and theory suggest that they are the result of the embryo's attempt to ensure a healthy pregnancy.

One of the world's leading researchers in this area feels that the unpleasant side effects of pregnancy are part of the body's attempt to store energy. Kirstin Uvnäs-Moberg is a physician and endocrinologist at the Karolinska Institute in Stockholm. After studying the hormones of digestion for ten years and going through four pregnancies herself, she felt compelled to combine these two areas of knowledge.

Uvnäs-Moberg began by looking at one of the most obvious facts about pregnant women: they get bigger. Part of their weight gain is due to the weight of the growing fetus, but about one third of the gained weight can be maternal fat. Evoluntionarily it makes sense that women and other female mammals would put on fat when pregnant. The growing baby needs an uninterrupted supply of energy and nutrients, and food has not always been (and still is not for many) as close as the supermarket or hamburger joint. Maternal fat stores give the baby an essential reservoir on which to draw. Even after pregnancy, stored fat can provide some of the steady energy supply necessary for breastfeeding.

Do pregnant women get heavier just because they eat more? Or could the increase in fat storage in pregnant women be the result of changes in digestive hormones, and therefore in gastrointestinal metabolism? Uvnäs-Moberg found that eating more is part of the reason for the weight gain, especially in mid and late pregnancy. But she also observed that most women start gaining weight at the beginning of pregnancy, even though many are feeling sick at that time and eating little (and when the embryo weighs almost nothing). Through their recent work, Uvnäs-Moberg and other scientists have determined that weight increases are indeed partly due to changes in metabolism, and the nausea, fatigue, and hunger may be part of those changes.

First of all, it helps to understand how hormones normally take part in the digestion process. When you eat, your stomach stretches and detects changes in acidity and the presence of nutrients. These signs tell your body to release hormones and other signaling molecules into the stomach, intestines, and bloodstream. Some of these signals mobilize the enzymes that break down the food for immediate use. Others work to store nutrients.

Unless the body is under stress, it normally treats most meals to a dose of the signaling molecules that create optimum conditions for energy storage. These signaling molecules—known as CCK (cholecystokinin), gastrin, and secretin—help digest food by increasing the production of stomach acids and keeping food in the stomach longer. They also boost the production of insulin, which pulls sugars out of the bloodstream and puts them in storage.

Uvnäs-Moberg has evidence that pregnancy tailors the body's responses to make digestion very efficient and promote energy storage. She and others have shown that, in pregnant women, the release of CCK is much higher than normal after meals. The nausea and heartburn of pregnancy may be due to these higher levels of CCK and other hormones, which keep the acid level in the stomach high and keep food from being emptied into the intestine.

Feeling faint and dizzy may come from the enhanced release of insulin that these hormones promote. The insulin pulls sugars, the body's main source of energy, out of the bloodstream and into storage. Suddenly, there is an energy shortage for working cells throughout the body.

This is a mild version of the sort of sugar crisis that diabetics go through occasionally when they get hypoglycemia after injecting insulin. It's as if your paycheck kept going into your savings account instead of your checking account—very quickly the checks you write would start bouncing and the bills would stop getting paid. That's why pregnant women are advised to keep eating small snacks so they can keep blood sugar levels up despite the action of insulin. Food in the stomach also helps to neutralize some of its excess acid.

In addition to these bodily effects, the digestive hormones can also affect the mind. Everyone has experienced the postprandial stupor that sets in after a good meal: this is also an effect of CCK. The hormone seems to induce a sleepy, tired state in the brain. This response probably helps all of us slow down and digest the food that we eat. In pregnancy, fatigue is probably yet another mechanism for forcing a pregnant woman to conserve energy and store it in the form of fat. In effect, pregnancy seems to put the body on an emergency energy savings plan, a sort of crash anti-diet. All the digestive machinery is revved up to pull the most energy out of food and store it; nausea, hunger, weight gain, and fatigue are the result.

The Benefits of Barfing

The side effects of pregnancy hormones are not all bad. Studies show that for one reason or another, pregnant women who don't ever feel nauseated are two to three times more likely to miscarry than women who do. But some scientists think that storing extra energy isn't the only reason for reduction in miscarriages in women who get morning sickness. These scientists believe that putting your stomach in knots can secure other benefits.

If foods are rotting or contain toxins they usually have strong flavors and smells. One theory of morning sickness is that nausea and vomiting steer women toward bland foods and away from toxins that could hurt the developing embryo. Sickness may be most common in the first trimester because that is when most of the embryo's limbs and vital organs are forming. Morning sickness, therefore, might be a beneficial adaptation that has arisen through evolutionary selection.

Another theory is that morning sickness forces an expecting woman to vary her diet. When one food is always associated with nausea, the eater can literally become sick of it in very short order. When this happens, she seeks out other types of food, and will therefore get the wide variety of vitamins and minerals that the embryo needs.

None of these theories about morning sickness necessarily excludes the others. Morning sickness may have originated because it has multiple benefits: making energy more available, promoting a balanced diet, and protecting the embryo against toxins at the same time. The bigger mystery is not so much what morning sickness can do in pregnancy, but why some women get very sick and others do not. Moreover, a woman can feel extremely ill during one pregnancy and feel fine during the next. And why don't other animals experience morning sickness, if these benefits could apply to all mammals? Scientists still have no answers to these questions.

Growing Within, Glowing Without

Although morning sickness can be the most dramatic side effect of pregnancy, people note many other changes. In pregnancy, a woman's hair doesn't fall out as often as before, giving her tresses a fuller, more lustrous look. Her skin exudes more oil, which can make it soft and healthy-looking, but can also lead to the first acne attacks since adolescence. Her face can take on a rosy glow due to the 25% increase in blood volume in her body and the dilation of capillaries under the skin. In order to keep blood pressure normal despite the flood of new blood, the blood vessels relax, warming the extremities and dissipating the extra heat created by the fetus. Hormones that stimulate pigment cells in the body can lead to the appearance of a line down the stomach and the "mask of pregnancy," a pigmented area on the face.

As the baby grows rapidly inside, it is awash in steroids and other hormones that promote growth. The surge in steroid hormones in the blood will also suppress inflammatory responses in the body. Women with injury-related arthritis may experience sudden relief from stiffness and pain. In order to make room in the pelvis and rib cage for the expanding baby, other released substances soften ligaments and allow bones to rearrange themselves.

Many believe that pregnancy can also make women better athletes after the baby's birth. Blood volume increases during pregnancy, and this higher blood volume, with its greater oxygen-carrying potential, can give women a permanent competitive edge if they keep it up by renewing training shortly after giving birth. (Exercising during pregnancy, however, is an individual decision to be made by a woman and her doctor.) Many women also believe the pain of childbirth teaches them how to cope with discomfort while performing their sport. During the 1992 Olympics in Barcelona, Dr. Craig Sharp, consultant physiologist to the British Olympic team, was told by Eastern European sports doctors that they liked their athletes to have one child, and preferably two, because it made them better competitors. "The East Germans told me women are psychologically toughened by childbirth, they discover how they can handle extreme discomfort," Sharp told a Reuters reporter.

Biological molecules aren't the only thing that the embryo gives to its mother. Strangely enough, actual cells from the embryonic tissues break off into the mother's bloodstream and circulate through her body. That means that embryonic cells are actually coursing through her veins. Scientists estimate that one in ten thousand of the cells in the bloodstream are actually fetal cells. Researchers are now able to identify these cells and cull them from blood samples. This could soon result in a diagnostic technique whereby doctors take a blood sample from the mother and separate out embryonic cells, then perform prenatal genetic tests using standard techniques without resorting to amniocentesis or chorionic villus sampling (CVS).

Chemical communication between mother and child goes both ways. Mothers pass oxygen, sugars, salts, vitamins, and minerals to their offspring, of course, but they also pass chemical messengers like stress hormones, small proteins, and antibody molecules across the barrier.

Sitting in the midst of all this traffic is an unappreciated magician: the placenta.

The Vital Link

For most people, the placenta is merely the afterbirth, an afterthought to pregnancy, and in the past scientists themselves have viewed the placenta as just an anchor for the umbilical cord and a barrier to separate the two blood supplies. But the placenta is in fact an extraordinary organ that does much more than passively filter out impurities and let nutrients pass through. In many ways, it is the choreographer and conductor of most of the pregnancy. It is a multiple organ system with the functions of the liver, kidneys, and endocrine glands. With its diverse production capacities, the placenta creates many of the hormones that keep the pregnancy going and help the embryo grow. The many loops and crevices enveloped by its outer skin offer an incredibly large surface area—about ten square yards (about the same space as the amount of driveway under a large car)—in order to let the required oxygen and glucose, carbon dioxide, and waste products pass from one being to the other. And at the end of pregnancy, it probably has a large role in starting labor.

In effect, the placenta is a living, complex symbiont that begins to establish itself in the womb before the embryo and leaves the womb after it. The placenta itself consumes about one third of the oxygen and glucose it receives and uses that energy to manufacture intricate molecules and shuttle the building blocks of life from mother to child. The placenta is like a beneficial parasite that stage-manages most of the changes involved in pregnancy and allows mother and child to coexist.

Though there is no evidence that dried or ground placenta can itself, as some cultures think, provide relief from medical problems, an understanding of how the placenta does its job may provide the basis for new medical treatments. And as immunologists struggle to answer the great mystery of how the half-foreign fetus and half-foreign placenta so successfully invade the mother's tissue, they may find the keys that would keep transplant patients from rejecting their new organs.

Landfall: The First Week

As described in the last chapter, sperm and egg combine to create the mother of all cells, the very first part of the new being. This single cell is more massive than any cell in the human body, just over 0.1 millimeters (about the thickness of a piece of typing paper). From the moment of its creation, this new creature will need food: the carbohydrates, proteins, fats, sugars, minerals, and trace metals necessary for life. Bringing home the groceries, therefore, is one of the primary jobs of the new being, a prerequisite to growth.

Virtually every bit of the first food the new being consumes will come from the mother's egg. The father's sperm delivered little more than a packet of genetic information. Food from the mother's egg will run out soon after fertilization, and the embryo will need a more direct link to bring home the bacon. The embryo makes this connection in a surprisingly violent manner.

Successful fertilizations usually occur far up in the fallopian tubes, less than twenty-four hours after the egg bursts from the ovaries. Immediately, the fertilized egg begins to copy its cellular machinery, and when the duplication process is complete some time during the second day after fertilization, the cell divides into two equal parts. These two cells will divide again to make a clump of four cells, which then divide to make sixteen cells, and so on. When the cells are too numerous to count, the being starts to resemble a berry and is therefore called a *morula,* the Latin word for mulberry.

During this time the cells are not in direct contact with the mother's tissue. For about three days, the speck of cells floats in fluid inside the fallopian tube. Microscopic hairs in the walls of the fallopian tube and the action of delicate muscles push the mite toward the uterus. The cell cluster probably gets a bit of nutrition from sugars and other molecules floating in the fluid around it, but there is no way to really get enough food to grow. This is why, although the cells are dividing, they're not growing. Every time a cell divides, the two new cells are half as big as the old one. At first, therefore, the whole ball of cells remains the size of the fertilized egg.

When the cell cluster emerges from the estuary of the fallopian tube on about the fifth day after fertilization, its cells have subdivided even more, and a hollow cavity of fluid has formed in its center. At this time the pinpoint-sized ball is still a preembryo; the few cells that will become the embryo itself are only a small bulge on one side of the sphere, and all other cells will be part of the embryo's support system—the placenta and the membrane that encloses it. Late in the sixth day after fertilization, the pod of cells, now called a blastocyst, drifts to the edge of the dark sea of uterine fluid and beaches itself on the spongy *terra nova* of the womb, its home for the next thirty-seven weeks.*

In order to burrow into the tissue, the cell cluster blasts its way in. It releases chemicals into the lining of the womb that make uterine cells burst. This blasting process does two things: it clears a niche for the preembryo to fit into, and it provides a first real meal for the cluster. The preembryo loads up on the contents of the exploded

---

*Marsupials like kangaroos can halt development at this stage. This allows them to conceive while already pregnant, holding the extra embryo in suspended animation until the current pregnancy ends.

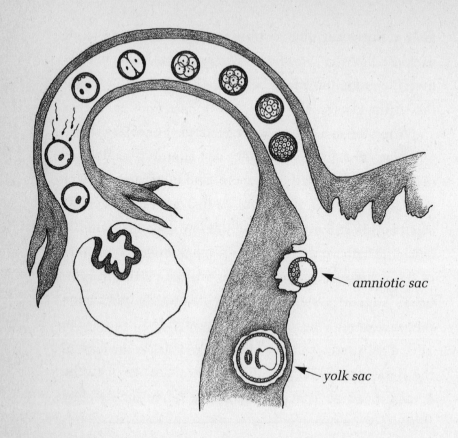

amniotic sac

yolk sac

uterine cells, making use of the proteins, fats, sugars, and other vital molecules. The preembryo's hole is a kind of wound: after excavating a place for itself, the blastocyst appears to be covered with a scab and a scar-like layer of maternal cells.

The intruder continues to release chemicals to attack the uterine tissue, and soon the mother's tiny blood vessels around it fall apart under the assault, springing holes like moth-eaten sweaters. Blood flushes out of these capillaries and seeps into cavities that have formed around the blastocyst, providing more food for its cells. The speck of a new being has received its first full meal from its mother and is replenished by the same blood that nourishes her.

Blood flows from the mother's ruptured capillaries into chambers in the thickening base of the preembryo, then flows back out to be picked up by the mother's veins. The base begins to extend outward in hair-like tendrils called microvilli, which infiltrate the mother's tissue like roots searching for water. (Some of these tendrils are taken when doctors perform the prenatal test called chorionic villus sampling [CVS].)

Eventually the microvilli and the thickening base of tissue will become a full-fledged placenta. But long before that happens, even from the moment the preembryo first touches the wall of the womb, it is transmitting a steady beat of chemical signals that have both beneficial and uncomfortable effects.

The Ties That Bond

The effects of the placenta can probably be felt even before the preembryo becomes embedded in the walls of the womb. Even as the smooth sphere of about 120 cells is free-floating out of the fallopian tube, many cells have begun to specialize and pump out chemical signals to the mother. In the first days after fertilization, the concentration of these chemical messengers is slight, and it is not until the preembryo actually becomes embedded in the womb that it begins to emit measurable chemical signals. In most cases it is a hormone called HCG (human chorionic gonadotropin) that first betrays the presence of the embedded preembryo. Doctors once used the rabbit test to look for this signal. In this test, a female rabbit was injected with fluid from a woman's body and any HCG present would cause the rabbit's ovaries to swell. For each test, a rabbit had to be sacrificed to check its ovaries (the phrase "the rabbit died" was synonymous with "I'm pregnant," although, in fact, the rabbit always died as part of the test). Now any woman can become a lab technician and test her urine for HCG in her own bathroom by using home pregnancy tests.

HCG and other hormones initiate an autopilot program for the mother's body. The hormones first prod the corpus luteum, the ovarian capsule that ejected the egg, to keep pumping out the steroid progesterone so that menstruation won't begin. After the first trimester, the placenta itself manufactures enough progesterone to keep the pregnancy going.

Molecules of HCG may also tell cells in the preembryo

to begin making other hormones. Many of these hormones are indistinguishable from the hormones produced by the pituitary gland in the mother's brain. These hormones also promote growth and development in the embryo. For instance, HCG itself may initiate the production of sex hormones in the developing reproductive glands of the embryo, hormones that themselves go on to have a broad range of effects on development.

The placenta is active in other ways. The barrier that the placenta sets up between fetal and maternal blood supplies not only lets oxygen, minerals, and small molecules flow through, it also actively selects and carries larger molecules to its opposite side. The largest molecules, such as antibodies, are actually swallowed whole by placental tissues, carried through and released into the fetal bloodstream in the late stages of pregnancy.

The placental tissues also produce several important proteins. At about ten weeks after fertilization, when placental tissues weigh about 50 grams, they are producing about 1.5 grams of protein per day. No organ in the adult body is so hardworking.

Perhaps the most amazing thing about the placenta, however, may be its ability to remain embedded in the wall of the womb.

Why Don't Our Mothers Reject Us?

Transplant surgeons know and fear the signs of tissue rejection. When they introduce a new heart into the chest of a patient with terminal heart disease, they watch and wait. If tissue rejection does occur, the patient becomes feverish and weak, and his kidneys and liver can begin to fail, as if the new heart represents a massive foreign infection. The immune cells that bring on this response, called T-cells, are part of what the military calls an IFF system—*Identification Friend or Foe.* T-cells constantly monitor all cells in the body for molecules that mark them as natives or intruders. The T-cells spot foreign markers on the surfaces of cells in the new heart and mobilize an attack. Without a heavy dose of drugs to suppress the immune system's attack, transplant patients' lives are threatened by the massive offensive the body mounts against the implant.

One of the most intriguing questions of modern immunology is why the implanted blastocyst, and later the placenta, is not rejected immediately by the mother. After all, the placenta and the fetus are half-foreign tissue—half the markers they carry are the father's—and half-foreign tissues are usually treated as fully foreign by the host. In addition, the implantation is not a gentle process. Cells from the blastocyst are in direct contact with maternal blood and antibodies. Yet without immunosuppressant drugs, the invading preembryo is able not only to survive, but to thrive and grow in what should be a hostile environment.

In a few women, about 1 in 600, the blastocyst *doesn't* implant. These women are unable to get pregnant, or they are able to get pregnant but suffer repeated miscarriages, usually in the first ten to twelve weeks of pregnancy. But most of the time embryos are able to avoid the alarm-and-attack system that protects us against microbial threats.

How does the blastocyst, and later the placenta, stave off rejection? The answer to this question could lead to new methods of preventing tissue rejection in transplant patients and of preventing the repeated miscarriages in women whose immune system does attack an implanting embryo.

In the past, some immunologists suspected that the uterus doesn't reject the fetus because it's an immunologically privileged site: perhaps it didn't respond to foreign tissue in the same way as most of the rest of the body does. This seemed entirely possible: the brain and the back of the eye are already known to be unusually accepting of foreign grafts.

Support for this idea came when scientists bred female mice that were immunologically sensitive to a male mouse's cell identification markers. The researchers then impregnated the female mice with the male's sperm. Because the females' sensitivity to the male's cell markers was increased, their immune systems should have caused an increased miscarriage rate. But the miscarriage rate didn't increase. This would seem to support the hypothesis that the womb is immunologically special. But further experimentation has shown that this is not so. When normal tissue is transplanted into the uterus, the mice reject it, showing that the uterus can be just as reactive as the rest of the body if the transplant is not an embryo.

Perhaps, then, maternal immune cells are preprogrammed to spare embryonic cells. Not so. Consider the phenomenon of Rh factor reactivity. When mother and offspring have different Rh factors in their bloodstreams, the mother's immune system can become sensitized to the opposite Rh factor. The mothers immune system can attack fetal cells when antibodies cross the placenta.

So how *do* most fetuses avoid being attacked? For the answer to this quandary, scientists first look to the front lines, the outside edge of the placenta called the trophoblast. Early in development, when the preembryo is implanting itself and for a few weeks after, the front wall of embryonic tissue makes itself as immunologically blank as possible. It doesn't make the usual markers that would identify it as foreign, and therefore it doesn't easily excite an immune reaction by the mother. The trophoblast also uses other tricks to impede rejection: it covers itself with HCG and releases steroid hormones, actions that suppress the reactivity of the immune system in the area of implantation.

These ruses make the trophoblast, and the embryo

inside it, particularly good at making itself at home wherever it happens to be. The best known example of this ability is an ectopic pregnancy, the dangerous condition in which the blastocyst implants itself not in the uterus but in a fallopian tube. Some embryos can drift out of the womb entirely, attaching themselves to folds of the bowel or intestines. Sadly, these pregnancies must be interrupted because the embryo can never develop properly outside the uterus and continuing the pregnancy can threaten the mother's life.

War No More

Eventually, though, the body's defensive system begins to recognize as foreign some of the implanted embryo. No tissue can be totally immunologically blank, and new attacks against the embryo are a danger long after it is firmly implanted in the womb. The way that the mother and embryo solve this problem belies conventional metaphors about the body's defensive system and makes the warlike talk of attacking and defending seem beside the point. Because the fetus and mother, appropriately enough, seem not to battle—they cooperate.

Even though the mother's immune system puts the embryo at risk, she also actively shields it from those same immune cells. For about a quarter of a century, scientists have known that some antibodies, the proteins that the immune system uses to recognize foreign bodies, can neutralize other antibodies and immune cells by latching on to them. It's like putting a little potato on the end of a fork so that the tines can't stab anything. When the business end of an antibody is blocked, it can't recognize the fetus as foreign. Scientists now think that, even as a mother's immune system begins to recognize the embryo as foreign, she begins producing anti-antibodies that inhibit her immune response to the fetus and placenta.

Even after the embryo has evaded most of the mother's immune responses, it still has to get by roving terminators called natural killer cells. Although they are not part of the classical immune system, natural killer cells are potent destroyers of cells that have become abnormal in some way, either by becoming cancerous or infected with a virus. No one knows exactly what sets natural killer cells on a murderous rampage, but it seems that embryonic cells have what it takes to invite an attack—probably because fetal cells look like abnormal maternal cells.

The fetus sends some sort of signal, perhaps through intermediaries, to special cells in the lining of the womb. These cells, called suppressor cells, seem to protect the fetus from the mother's natural killer cells, says the discover of the suppressor cells, Professor David Clark of McMaster University in Hamilton, Ontario, Canada. Trouble may occur when maternal suppressor cells don't do their job properly. Women who repeatedly suffer miscarriages may be having difficulties bringing the pregnancy to term because their suppressor cells aren't deactivating the natural killer cells, says Clark.

Oddly enough, Clark believes, the very foreignness of the embryonic cells may be what triggers the suppressor cells to begin working at the beginning of pregnancy. The foreign markers arouse some part of the immune system, which then *activates* the suppressor cells. The suppressor cells in turn stop the attacks of the natural killer cells. Clark and other scientists theorize that repeated miscarriages could be the result of markers on the fetal cells that don't look foreign *enough*. It's possible that if, by the luck of the draw, the father and the mother share markers that are too similar, the suppressor cells aren't activated and don't protect the fetus from the mother's natural killer cells.

The whole theory that the immune system is the cause of some miscarriages is controversial. Some scientists feel that genetic or developmental abnormalities, or the mother's poor health, are the real reasons for miscarriages. However, some scientists are pressing ahead with a therapy based on the idea that defective suppressor cells are the true cause.

Some medical researchers have tried giving women who have repeated miscarriages a dose of the father's white blood cells. This treatment incites an immune reaction against the paternal cells and presumably activates the suppressor cells that protect the fetus. Other researchers, such as David Clark, find that any activation of the maternal immune system seems to turn on these protective mechanisms. Some doctors claim an 80 percent success rate with these techniques, although other researchers claim that most of these women would have had a normal pregnancy anyway if they were given the medical support and counseling that came with the immunotherapy.

One offshoot of this work may be a clearer understanding of cancer. Since the defensive cells that protect the body against viruses and cancer cells are the same ones that are suppressed in pregnancy, cancer cells might be using the same tricks the fetus uses to avoid detection and rejection, Clark says. After all, every cell in the body has many genes that lie dormant. Some of these genes, if activated, could allow cancer cells to mimic the fetus, fooling the body into thinking that they belong there. If this is true, medical researchers might learn how to teach the body *intolerance* of cancer cells, just as they are now trying to teach the body *tolerance* of embryonic cells.

Womb to Grow

As these few dozen cells in the embryo multiply, they alter not only a mother's immune response, but also her digestive processes, her blood chemistry, her emotional reactions, even the sinews and tendons that hold her body together. They also subdue a basic drive to protect herself against organisms that aren't part of her. And the embryo subverts this process precisely, subtly tinkering with the behavior of the usually mercenary immune cells so that they still attack and destroy disease-causing organisms, leaving the fetus untouched. Transplant surgeons can only envy the embryo's amicable status as resident alien in the womb, as medical science continues to use the chemical equivalent of sledgehammers to suppress the whole immune system for other tissue grafts.

With such powerful forces at work, it should be no surprise that pregnancy is not always a joyful celebration of life. Growing is hard, and the wash of developmental hormones and the demands of the embryo can cause uncomfortable side effects. Nature's response to a mother's complaints is "So be it." After all, from an evolutionary viewpoint, it doesn't matter if pregnancy is easy for the mother—as long as she survives it. In fact, a little discomfort may be just the ticket to get her attention.

At no time is this attention more important than during the first fifth of the pregnancy, the month and a half when the embryo changes from ameboid sphere to miniature human.

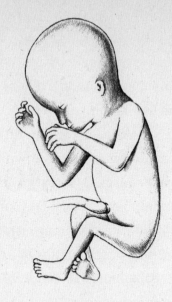

actual size

THE THIRD MONTH

(Weeks 9–13 after conception;
weeks 11–15 after LMP)

In the third month, the fetus floats in the salty amniotic fluid of the uterus. With its nodding head and bent legs and toes, it looks very much like an astronaut sleeping in space. The tough umbilical cord coils between his belly and the placenta. During this month, the baby's neck grows further and straightens. At the same time, the eyelids grow over the eyes, closing them until they open again in the sixth month. The baby's hands and feet are well developed, and in the ninth week he starts to grow fingernails and toenails. By the end of the month, the little sprite is able to grab, kick, and curl his toes; he may even scratch himself with his new nails.

One of the primary markers of the start of this fetal period is the growth of bone. Although a very few bones began to form in the second month, bone growth begins in earnest during the third month.

Perhaps the biggest change in the third month is that we can differentiate the girls from the boys. Until the 9th week there is no apparent difference in the external genitals of boys and girls: they both look like boys. Both have a creased bump that is the phallus. In boys in the 9th week of development (11th week after LMP), the testis releases a burst of male hormones, the crease fuses and disappears, and the phallus stays. In girls, nothing genitally dramatic happens during week 9, but over the next few weeks the crease stays and the phallus retracts to become a clitoris.

At week 11 the baby will open his mouth, and if a finger brushes his mouth he might suck it. By week 12 he begins swallowing amniotic fluid. Over the course of the month the fetus just about doubles in size to nearly 9 centimeters—3½ inches—from the head to rump. The baby's legs are folded and hard to measure at this point, but the total height of the baby is about 13 centimeters (over 5 inches). During this month, the amniotic sac has grown from the size of a small plum to that of a large orange. At the end of the 13th week (15th week after LMP), he weighs 60 grams (just over two ounces). By the end of the month the fetus is moving vigorously, although mothers can't feel movement until next month at the earliest.

THREE

FROM BLOB TO BABE—THE FIRST FIFTY DAYS

IN THE VERY FIRST MOMENTS AFTER BIRTH, AFTER THE final, sweaty push has produced a squalling, writhing package, most parents have an overwhelming urge to know: Is the baby all right? Does he or she have two arms and legs, ten fingers, ten toes?

The overwhelming majority of babies are, in fact, just fine. Everything seems to be in the right place, the fingers are fingers, the toes, toes. And when the parents see that all is in place, they marvel at the tininess of this new person. They wonder at the perfect little hands, the dimples at the knuckles, the teensy fingernails lined up like match sticks. To think that such a being could grow from nearly nothing!

Parents have undoubtedly felt these emotions through the ages, but these feelings have also fueled intense analytical thought by philosophers and scientists. That is because the wonder of those tiny hands and perfect eyes strikes at a central question in science: How are we formed from the raw material, the clay, of the world? How are water, carbohydrates, proteins, and assorted minerals and metals able to come together to form such a complex structure? In the last two centuries, scientists have rejected the idea that a baby grows out of a microscopic human that is already in the sperm or egg and the question has become more pointed. If we start as a collection of cells, how does each cell know where to go as we grow? Why are we shaped as we are, and how is that shape reproduced? If we start out as a microscopic ball of cells, why don't we end up as a big ball of cells?

Perhaps most amazing of all, these changes take place very quickly. In the first fifty days of pregnancy, that tiny ball of cells will change to a little person, with a place for thousands of different types of cells, and every type of cell in its place. While during the second day after conception the embryo looks like two egg yolks jammed together at the bottom of a glass, by the fiftieth day the heart, liver, brain, bones, and blood are packaged in arms, legs, head, and trunk. The heart beats and the limbs move. Signals zing along nerves and two eyes are set in a childlike face. These first fifty days hold the most incredible physical transformation of our lives, a metamorphosis from blob to babe.

How does this transformation occur? The mysterious change is becoming less mysterious all the time. Scientists studying the development of humans and other vertebrates whose embryos develop similarly, have discovered a complex ballet, a dance of cells that move, mix and multiply in time with a chemical beat. The choreography of the developing embryo during these seven weeks displays a repertoire of the themes that are not only vital for development but remain important throughout our lives. And scientists have found that, as in any good drama, this critical period of becoming contains movement, expression, change, wisdom, and even death.

Baby in a Compact Disk

The overture to this drama is the early developmental events that were described in the last chapter. As the berry-like morula floats down the fallopian tubes and then grows into a hollow ball of cells on the fourth day, the sub-group of cells that will become the embryo is still clustered among the other non-embryo cells in the ball. Most of the cells that have come from the egg are support cells—necessary for existence in the womb but ultimately expendable after birth. The cells of the embryo haven't yet separated themselves out and become an identifiable entity. When the hollow ball implants itself in the wall of the womb on the sixth day, it begins thickening at its base.

As the first week of development ends, the sun rises on a new land: an oval island of cells, the embryo itself, a disk sandwiched between two bodies of fluid, the amniotic sac and the yolk sac. The amniotic sac, which will eventually surround the baby completely, is now just a small bubble. Next to the amniotic sac is the balloon-like "yolk sac," which actually contains no yolk, but seems to provide some nutrition. Like the yolk in fertilized bird eggs, it provides a surface on which the embryo can begin to form. At this point, the embryo is grayish and translucent. With no blood and no pigment, it's as clear as a jellyfish.

It is this island that will transform itself within the first fifty days. How? To help us understand this change, we will use a very un-babylike metaphor. Because, in some ways, a pink and plucky baby is like a big, brash, American city. And the developmental history of the embryo island mirrors the history of an island city: Manhattan.

When seen from the top of the Empire State Building, New York City seems miraculous for existing at all. Every day, the sun rises on a city that is already on the move as trucks deliver goods from crowded produce, meat, and flower markets. Phone lines and satellite links are already teeming with information from European and Japanese markets as the stock exchanges prepare for their daily financial frenzy. As light begins to creep down the walls of the buildings, the tires and shoes that tread on the still shaded streets below carry hundreds of thousands of beings on their journey to work. Throughout the day, trucks and trains lift tens of thousands of tons of food into the city, while trucks and barges carry out hundreds of thousands of tons of the city's garbage and detritus.

How does the city survive? Any idea of planning these activities centrally, through one office, is absurd. It would be a logistical nightmare. Instead, the city survives (and those who ♥ New York would say it thrives) because citizens look out for their own interests, pursue their own goals.

Each human is somewhat like a city, and every cell like a citizen. We survive because billions of cells do their separate jobs independently, but in a concerted fashion. Each of us is a community of cells, and the events that occurred in the development of another community, New York City, are parallel to our own.

So how did New York City develop? After the Dutchman Peter Minuit bought Manhattan for about twenty-four dollars in cloth, trinkets, and beads (thereby completing the first and last truly great deal in New York real estate history), he began building the city. But it is highly doubtful that he said, "In three hundred and fifty years we will have a population of several million on the Island of Manhattan, and buildings one hundred times as large as the tallest tree." Instead, the town grew within a certain framework because there was logic to its growth, a logic based on the placement of Fort Amsterdam and the canal that is now Broad Street at the southern end of the island. Once the first structures were built, the founders used what had been built before as a reference: they placed new buildings near old ones. They built new streets to continue the grid that was settled on earlier. In other words, the way the town acquired new structures was dictated by the placement of previous structures.

It turns out that our development is analogous.

At day eight, the embryo island seems featureless and unmarked. But like a new land being settled, the terrain of the embryo island is already mapped and divided. The island is made of two flat layers of cells. The bottom stratum of cells, those next to the yolk sac, is slated to become the layer of "inner skin": the lining of the throat, the stomach, the intestines, lungs, and various internal organs. In the top layer, next to the amniotic fluid, are the cells that will grow to become most of the body. This layer is divided into fields of cells, each already predestined to become certain general types of tissue.

One scientist, using a slightly different metaphor, said that if an embryo developed into a house, the top layer would become the exterior paint, shingles, and wiring; the lower layer would become the plumbing, appliances, and the interior paint; and the middle layer would become everything else.

On the 16th day after conception, just as the menstrual period is first being missed, every embryo begins a process so vital that the British biologist Louis Wolpert likes to say it is the most important event in every life. It is a folding of the flat sheet of cells to determine the basic shape the baby will build on until he is born, the shape we all have for all of our lives. This folding makes us grow not into a big blob, nor a big disk of cells, but into a person with a head and rear and a passageway running from between the two through a tubular trunk. It's a basic plan that most animals, and all vertebrates, possess, and it's worked well through hundreds of millions of years.

The first visible sign of folding occurs at the edge of the island of cells. A small dimple begins to form, which lengthens into a crack. Cells flow toward each other along the surface of the disk, and then flow downward into the crack, like Jell-O on a slotted spoon. The cells flow into the space between the two layers and fill it out. Down into the interior of the embryo go all the cells destined to become internal tissues—bones, muscle, tendons, and tooth pulp. (It is interesting, though, that the tooth's enamel comes from the top layer, the same layer that supplies the skin. This may finally give meaning to the phrase, "The skin of your teeth.") Over a three-day period, half the disk moves down into the groove.

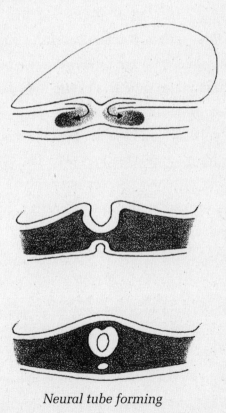

Neural tube forming

When the cells destined to become the middle layer have disappeared down the crack it is roofed over: At the beginning of the fourth week the top sheet joins midway down the groove and the two sides are melded as if two invisible zippers were moving outward from the middle to the ends. The hollow duct that is created becomes the spinal cord, the brain, and the net of nerves that lace the body. Very rarely, the ends of this tube don't close completely, which results in spina bifida, a birth defect. In recent years scientists have discovered that an adequate supply of folic acid, a B vitamin, in the mother's diet at this stage of pregnancy can reduce the risk of spina bifida.

While the neural tube is closing, the edges of the embryonic disk grow downward and together, pinching off part of the yolk sac and creating the tube that will become the throat, lungs, and intestines. The flat disk of the embryo has now become a short being, with a head and rear, a back and a front, and the two critical ducts that will process food, air, and nerve signals.

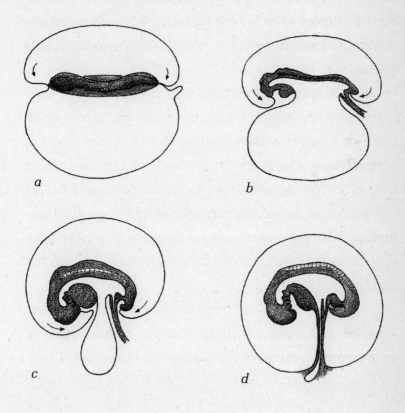

a

b

c

d

Origami Mommy

This first shaping of the embryo employs the three essential processes that will be used again and again as the fetus builds itself into the form it has at birth: folding, cell migration, and cell instruction. We'll start by looking at why folding is so essential.

By following inborn instruction for bending and folding, the embryo doesn't have to "know" what shape it's finally supposed to have, and every cell doesn't have to "know" exactly where it is supposed to end up. Only a few cells at the folding point have to be induced to bend. This way, complex structures can arise through simple, step-by-step instruction, just as a megalopolis like New York City can arise through step-by-step additions to what has already been built.

Another example of how this works is origami, the Japanese art of paper folding. Origami artists make the most exquisite, intricate objects through the repeated folding of single sheets of paper. Think about the origami swan. Creating this paper bird without folding would require a lot of cutting and taping in accordance with elaborate instructions—and what most people would probably end up with is an ugly duckling instead of a swan. Most people can, however, fold paper in clean, straight lines and come up with an object that is respectably swan-like.

Folding is used throughout early development to shape the embryo. One example has already been mentioned: the folding of the embryonic disk to make the spinal cord. Another example is the formation of the eye. During the third week of development, part of the tissue that will become the brain extends toward the surface tissue of the embryonic head. This pre-brain tissue causes cells in the skin to contract toward it. One side of each cell contracts, making the whole surface pucker and sink inward, forming a hole where each eye will be. Then like the future spinal cord, the cells at the edge of this invagination pull together and roof over the hole. This newly formed bubble then breaks away from the surface layer of cells to become the future lens of the eye. The neural outgrowth that began this process spreads around the lens to become the future retina, where light is detected and encoded in nerve signals pulsing toward the brain.

Yet another example of folding tissue is the heart, which starts as a straight tube. In the fourth week, this tube begins to bunch up and fold over on itself. Where folds touch, openings form in the heart wall. In other places, the folding process pinches off and closes the original tube. In the end, the tube has been transformed into a multichambered heart that functions as a muscular pump.

Face Facts

Just what *is* that little groove and the two ridges running between your upper lip and nose *for*? The truth is that the groove, called the philtrum, doesn't have a purpose: it's an artifact, a wrinkle left behind in the folding of the face. The construction of the face is a good subject for study—partly because everyone knows exactly what a face looks like, and because it is hard to imagine how such a complex thing arises out of a few folds of skin.

The most dramatic changes in the process of making a face begin about day 26, late during the fourth week, and continue until the embryo becomes a fetus at the end of the third month. The face begins as a series of folds—four pleats called arches—separated by grooves. (In fish embryos, very similar folds will become gills, but in humans they become the forehead, the upper and lower jaws, the ears, and organs of the throat.) At first these arches seem to have no more shape than a stack of pancakes, but this is exactly how the great beauties of the ages, from Helen of Troy to Sean Connery, got their start. The first recognizable features to emerge are the primitive eye (which we have already discussed), and a curved cushion of cells around two holes that will become the nostrils.

During the fifth week, these cushions begin to descend into the first arch. Meanwhile, the edges of the third and

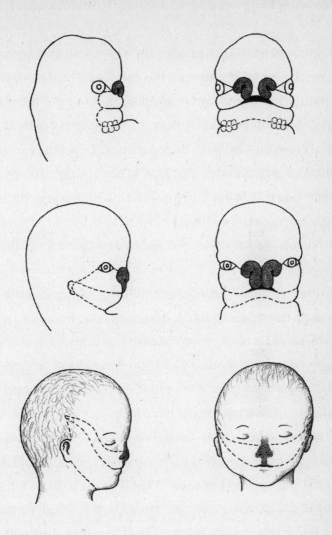

fourth arch begin to fold and crumple themselves, forming little ridges, and the eye spots start becoming rounded and look more like eyeballs. In the sixth and seventh weeks, the cushions around the nose arch widen to form a mouth. The ridged and crumpled edges of the third and fourth arch, left behind by the rapidly dividing cells at the front of the face, take up their position as proto-ears.

By the eighth week, the face is beginning to be recognizably that of a baby. The rounded cushions have become a nose, the eyes have moved forward to the front of the face and are closer together, the ears have moved up to the sides of the head.

When all the folding and melding is done, little remains of the original folds. The nips and tucks of tissue have been seamlessly sewn together. But artifacts can still be seen, even in the adult face. The flaring skin around the nostrils, the openings of the mouth, ears and nose, and the philtrum mark where folds have been.

On a cat's face these artifacts can be seen more clearly. The rings around each nostril are easily visible, still separated by a vertical groove. The first arch hasn't fused smoothly with the nose, and there is a vertical gap running from the mouth to the nose. In some humans, in about 1 in 1,000 people, this fold doesn't fuse smoothly either, resulting in a cleft lip (and inside the mouth, a cleft palate).

On-the-Job Training

By folding sheets of cells, the embryo can change simple shapes into complex ones. And yet, there is another extremely critical process that takes place in the developing embryo, not only in the face, but everywhere in the body. Cells are taught their jobs. Again, a few simple instructions make it possible to establish the huge variety of jobs that cells must do.

To return to the example of New York City, the founding residents probably found it necessary to be able to do many jobs. Someone might have to know how to farm eggs, do light carpentry and brew beer. As the city developed, skills were passed on to succeeding generations and split up so that each individual had one job—and some people have jobs that were never dreamed of when the city was founded.

Cells in the early embryo, too, are at first relatively unspecialized. Then some cells are instructed to divide quickly and others to divide slowly. Some learn to function as part of a taste bud and others become part of a muscle. Just as sons and daughters of New York City residents might take over the family business, the instructions that cells get take them and their descendants down certain career paths. The descendants often receive the training to specialize further, but they almost never go backward and become generalists again.

But there is some flexibility in this plan. In New York City a bright child might become an auto mechanic if he is brought up in one environment and a mechanical engineer if he is brought up in another. In the same way, cells are given certain potentials by their parental cells. But what they become depends both on that potential and on who their neighbors are as they mature. How are cells shaped by their environment? What do their neighbors whisper in their ears as they grow?

In recent years, scientists have been tapping into those messages, learning how cells are taught to behave as they do. They are learning why cells follow one career path and not another*. Instruction requires that cells communicate,

---

*Actually, since all cells have the same genetic machinery, each cell already "knows" how to do any job in the body. Therefore, special abilities are actually *selected* from a catalog of possible programs rather than *taught* from scratch.

that messages pass from the teachers to the pupils. Who's doing the teaching?

One possible candidate for such a communicator is the cell-adhesion molecules (CAMs) that clothe each cell and tell the other cells their status. (CAMs also bind the cells together—without them we would be pools of ooze.) But a more likely source of instruction are diffusible molecules that drift between cells like words in the air. Ironically, in the 1980s, just as researchers were discovering how these "instructor" molecules probably work, a series of tragedies served to focus public attention on the action of one of them.

Beauty and Beastliness

In 1982, the United States Food and Drug Administration (FDA) approved the sale of a new acne medication. To most people acne seems a trivial nuisance, more a threat to someone's ego than to their life. However, some people are afflicted by a type of acne so severe that cysts form under the skin and leave scars and pockmarks in their wake. This deep, cystic acne often doesn't respond to standard therapies, and it inflicts physical and emotional scars that can last a lifetime. Researchers discovered, however, that the drug Accutane was so effective against deep acne that just one treatment could completely clear it up. Even the usually staid Merck manual, which catalogues almost every disease and treatment known to medicine, proclaims that Accutane "revolutionized" the treatment of acne. For sufferers of cystic acne, the discovery of Accutane was miraculous.

There was only one caveat: in standard, pre-approval tests, Accutane was found to cause birth defects in lab animals. Although no one knew if Accutane would cause defects in humans, the FDA considered the possible danger and required that doctors prohibit Accutane's use in pregnant women. The FDA also advised that doctors give a pregnancy test to prospective Accutane users and warn women of the dangers of becoming pregnant while they were taking the drug.

Unfortunately, many of the women who need acne medication are teenagers or in their early twenties—prime fertility years. Some doctors, too, were not careful to make sure women understood the dangers of Accutane, and sometimes they didn't certify that women weren't already pregnant when they began taking the drug. By 1983, reports were coming in that babies exposed to Accutane in the womb were arriving in delivery rooms with tiny heads, shrunken faces, and other problems.

This news inspired years of controversy, with some calling for the removal of Accutane from the market. Ultimately, the FDA decided to continue to allow doctors to prescribe Accutane—in part because there was no drug to replace it—but changed the packaging to provide a stronger warning. The agency also recommended strict new precautions, such as requiring women to take a pregnancy test and wait a month before beginning therapy with the drug.

How does Accutane cause such havoc in the developing embryo? The trouble is probably the result of mistaken identity. Accutane, also called isotretinoin, likely resembles one of the body's natural signaling molecules. These natural chemicals, the morphogens (literally, "shape makers"), tell cells how to change and what to become. Accutane probably does its dirty work by drowning out the subtle instructions travelling from one embryonic cell to another.

What might the natural morphogen look like? Accutane is a chemical cousin of vitamin A, so the morphogen is probably in the same family of chemicals, scientists reasoned. Little did they know that the chemical they were looking for was close at hand, virtually next door to the scene of the crime. The scientists found it by studying another important development of the first fifty days: the growth of the arms and legs.

Mirror, Mirror

After the basic body is formed and the head, heart, and the spinal column are all clearly laid out, the embryo looks like a minute tadpole only five millimeters long, about the width of a pencil eraser. At this point, two bumps begin to form on the each side of the body just below the heart, and another two near its tail-end. These are called limb buds, an appropriate name for the nubs that will bloom into exquisite arms, hands, legs, and feet. Scientists discovered only in the late 1980s how the basic plan for the developing limbs unfold, how the limb stalks grow out just so far and then blossom into the delicate collection of muscles, tendons, and bones that can eventually dance *en point* or play the piano.

Scientists found that the trick for shaping the limbs is to let cells know just what position they occupy. If each cell knows its position, it can then be programmed to do the job required at that spot. In humans, if cells are on the top of the arm they start training to become part of a bulging bicep. If they are farther out, they may begin to form the fine muscles that control the fingers.

There seem to be two ways to tell cells what position they are in: one way to let them know if they are on top or on the bottom, and another to let them know how far out on the limb they are. The scientists found that the first instruction, for top or bottom, seems to be emitted by a little patch of skin just below the limb bud. The chemical shape-maker seems to spread from this patch into the outlying tissue, getting more dilute the farther it gets from its source. Chick embryos develop wings in the same way, so a lot of what we know about the process of limb development comes from studying them. Louis Wolpert found that an odd thing happened when he duplicated this patch, called an organizer, above the developing chick wing, just opposite the natural organizer. Instead of a normal wing, the limb developed into a double wing, a mirror image with two tops and no bottom. This seemed to happen because the two patches created two areas of high concentration of the morphogen. Therefore, the two edges of the wing thought they were the top edge.

But what is this chemical that diffuses away from the organizer? What is the morphogen? In his engrossing book *The Triumph of the Embryo,* Wolpert describes how he bumped into another researcher who happened to mention that he was using a chemical that had an interesting effect on cell development. Wolpert tried implanting a small bead soaked with the chemical into the spot where he had previously sewn the duplicate organizer. The results were the same: the embryo grew exactly the same double wing.

The chemical was retinoic acid, or retin-A, the other acne medication in the vitamin A family.

This experiment and others like it have gone a long

way toward showing that retinoic acid, or a chemical very much like it, may be an important chemical for shaping limbs in developing animals, including humans. Scientists have shown that the patch of organizer cells from one species organize developing limbs just as well in another. This suggests that the chemical that is released is the same in all animals.

Working by the Clock

The second lesson that cells in the limbs must be taught is how far out on the limb they are. As mentioned previously, this determines whether they will become part of the elbow or hand, knee or foot. The leading theory about how this happens is that there is a zone of rapidly dividing cells, called the progress zone, near the end of the limb bud. Like a group of steelworkers who build a skyscraper floor by floor, the cells in the progress zone put down layer after layer of the growing limb. What part of the limb each layer of cells becomes seems to be determined by how long they stay in the progress zone. In other words, there's something like a timing mechanism that tells cells how long they've been in the progress zone and what type of cells are needed there, just as steelworkers know what floor they're working on and what sort of structures they should build.

Cell Suicide

Cities that have been around for a while are rebuilt on their own ruins. This fact is obvious in cities like Rome, where the remains of ancient buildings are regularly dug up. But in almost every modern city, building sites have also been razed and rebuilt many times over the years. Just as demolition is an important part of the building of any city, so it is in the body: Destruction is an important part of development.

To sculpt the final contours of the body, cells must die. As the hands and legs approach their correct shape in the sixth week, they widen into little paddles that will become the hands and feet. The paddles grow ridges that will become the fingers and toes. And then, in the seventh week, the cells between these ridges die.

This mass cell death allows the fingers and toes to be independent; without the death of this tissue we would have webbed fingers and toes. In fact, children are very occasionally born with such webbing, a sign that cells failed to die as they should.

Even more surprising is that these cells aren't killed off—they commit suicide. Scientists believe that these cells are *programmed* to die after they have served their purpose. Such programmed cell death seems to be an important part of development, not only in the hands and feet but also in the mouth, the nose, the brain, and other places in the body. Since discovering programmed cell death, scientists have begun to search for diseases that may be caused by cells that accidentally activate a suicide program in adult life. Some brain diseases, for instance Huntington's disease, seem to be the result of unexplained death of cells in critical parts of the brain. If researchers find that these brain cells are killing themselves during development, they may be closer to finding a way to prevent harmful cell suicide in adults.

The Untutored Cell

By the end of the eighth week, the tiny embryo, an inch and a quarter long, has changed: from a flat disk of cells it has grown and folded into a little nub of a creature that's beginning to look like a baby. Through the migration of small groups of cells and the growing and bending sheets of tissue, the embryo has acquired a complex, human form.

Through the process of differentiation—individual cell instruction—the liver begins to function as a liver and the skin as skin. Under the influence of chemicals and other agents, the cells in the body have become progressively more specialized in their work. At the eight-cell stage of development, each cell could, on its own, create a whole new embryo. By the time the 8th week is reached, however, most cells are stuck with a narrow range of duties and rely on each other for survival. Once a skin cell, always a skin cell: it can't go back to its salad days when it was young and could become anything. That's why we can't clone ourselves—the cells in our bodies became irreversibly specialized long ago.

Right now, a great deal of research is devoted to finding and using stem cells, which are relatively unspecialized and can grow into many different kinds of cells. The big emphasis now is on blood stem cells, which live inside our bone marrow and produce all the blood and immune cells. Chemotherapy or radiation therapy for cancer wipes out this population of stem cells, and bone marrow donors are needed to reestablish the population. Unfortunately, finding a donor with a matching type of stem cell is difficult, often impossible. Peter Gale, an oncologist in Los Angeles, has pointed out that the blood in the umbilical cord after birth is rich in stem cells and that perhaps we should harvest and store cord blood for babies in case they (or relatives) later get cancer. A few blood storage companies are now offering to store cord blood for an annual fee.

In the future we may be able to learn how cells know where they are and how they learn the jobs they do. Then it may be possible to perform medical feats that would now be considered miracles. Physicians might grow as much blood as they need in laboratory flasks and custom-design cells that fight diseases. They might grow new organs to replace failing livers, kidneys, or hearts from slivers of tissue. Scarless surgery might result if scientists could learn how the fetus fuses sheets of folding tissue without leaving a mark. Eventually, some researchers hope, primitive cells might be exposed to the precise sequence of chemicals necessary to make them bud into new arms or legs on the stumps of lost limbs.

Many scientists are convinced that these treasures are waiting to be discovered along the scientific trail they are currently cutting, a trail winding toward the most fundamental questions about how we develop and how humans evolved. In order to find these rewards, scientists must delve deep into the very machinery of life. They will have to understand the workings of the jungle of genetic blueprints contained in the thicket of twisted vines called DNA.

actual size

THE FOURTH MONTH

(Weeks 14–17 after conception;

weeks 16–19 after LMP)

In this month, the fetus's body starts growing a fine hair called lanugo (from the Latin *lana* for fine wool), starting on his eyebrows and upper lip. By the middle of the next month, his body will be completely covered with the downy hairs. In furry animals these hairs stay and grow through birth, but in humans the lanugo gradually disappears late in the pregnancy from everywhere except the scalp and the eyebrows. Even much of the scalp and eyebrows can be shed shortly after birth, leaving a bald or patchy down before permanent hair comes in.

The fetus's body is also beginning to catch up with his head in growth. During the third month, the baby's head was about half his body length, but during this month it drops to about one-third of the length of his body. By birth, the length of the head will be about one-fourth that of the body.

While the rate of growth during this month and the next is very rapid, the gain in weight is still slow. This is partly because the baby has not started adding the volumes of ordinary fat that bulk him up for birth. One kind of fat he is adding, though, is a special type called brown fat. Brown fat has that color because it is rich with cell structures that can turn the fat directly into energy to keep the baby warm. Most stores of white fat have to be transported out of the cells in order to tap their energy.

By this time, the nerve cells in the brain have finished dividing and have reached their maximum number. Now the number of cells will decline as the brain begins the nerve pruning that shapes brain function. During this period, nerve cells also begin to form the fatty covering called myelin, which makes signals travel faster and further on their trips to and from the brain.

The fetus continues to move, although his movements are so subtle that his mother probably won't feel them. From the 12th to 16th week, his diaphragm goes up and down as if he's breathing—which, of course, he's not—but then, for no known reason, this movement disappears until the third trimester. By the end of the month, the baby is about 25 centimeters long (10 inches) from head to heel, and curled into a ball 15 centimeters (6 inches) across. He weighs about half a pound.

FOUR

GENE GENIES

AT 9:03 P.M. ON THE EVENING OF JUNE 21, 1982, DIANA, Princess of Wales, gave birth to an infant boy. The news of the birth of an heir to the throne set off a national rejoicing, and the next day Queen Elizabeth II came to visit her grandson for the first time. As the Queen of England beheld the likely future King William V, Lord of Northern Ireland, England and Scotland, Protector of the Faith, Emperor of Overseas Dominions, she reportedly remarked dryly: "Thank goodness he hasn't got ears like his father."

The Queen's inspection of her grandson for evidence

of his father's royal jug ears is an example of an ancient ritual. Everyone always wants to know whose features the baby bears. Does she have her father's hair? Does he have his mother's eyes? Or does the tyke bear a resemblance to Alfred E. Newman, *Mad* magazine's dish-eared cover boy? As children grow, relatives and friends also keep an eagle eye out for personality traits that seem to be gleaned from family members. Does he have his father's gregariousness? His mother's wit? His uncle's temper?

People have an undying and understandable fascination with genetic traits. There is something almost spooky about seeing a piece of yourself in someone else, or in seeing something you thought was unique to your spouse unexpectedly reveal itself in your child. There is a visceral satisfaction in knowing that part of you will exist outside of yourself, will extend you beyond your own place and time. In addition, there is something strangely relieving in seeing personality traits (even bad ones) carry over into offspring. They imply that your love of music or your aggravating perfectionism is somehow part of your bedrock foundation, that any excesses you undertake in pursuit of these traits are unavoidable ("Hey, I can't mow the lawn—I was born to play the accordion and I've just got to do it now"). It justifies and relieves you of some responsibility for your actions and seems to grant you a certain noblesse oblige in life.

For these reasons, genetic theories and explanations

have been prone to abuse. The seductive quality of genetics is that it seems so simple on the surface and appears to offer easy (and easily understandable) explanations for the way the world is, with clear-cut prescriptions for change. Why does wealth seem to stay in certain circles? It is more comfortable for people with wealth to look to genetic inheritance rather than the fiscal sort ("It's breeding"). Why are some people acid-tongued and abusive? To blame genetics seems to relieve them of responsibility for changing ("It's just the way I am"). At their worst, genetic theories have been twisted and misapplied to justify massive programs of sterilization and genocide.

Since the dark ages of genetic science and eugenics, scientists have learned volumes about how genes actually work. New work has allowed researchers to focus on exactly how the genetic genies cast their spells on developing cells. New statistical methods have enabled them to study previously untapped populations and begin to quantify exactly how much specific charter traits owe their existence to genetic influences and how much these traits are influenced by the environment. In most scientific circles, bad science (and evangelical advocacy of suspect social and racial theories) based on genetics have given way to a quieter and much more reasoned science. Over the last twenty years, researchers have mounted an impressive body of evidence about genetic influences on our personalities.

Alongside the expanding work on how genes shape

our personality, scientists have been studying how genes shape us physically. This research, although not widely discussed, is turning out to be some of the most significant research in modern biological science.

Genetic Packaging

Until forty years ago, no one knew much about what a gene actually looked like. People have long known that children got some looks and personality from their parents, and animal breeding and domestication was based on the principle of collecting desirable traits through selective breeding. It wasn't until just over a hundred years ago, however, that the Austrian monk Gregor Mendel came upon the principle that certain traits were carried by packets of information (genes) from each parent, and some of these packets were stronger (dominant genes) while others were weaker (recessive genes). Dominant genes (say, for tallness in pea plants) when mixed with recessive genes (say, shortness) would always win; the resulting pea plants would all be tall. But what no one could say at that time is what these packages were, and how they carried this information.

In the 1940s and 1950s, scientists zeroed in on deoxyribonucleic acid (DNA) as the molecule that genes are made of, and in 1953 James Watson and Francis Crick dis-

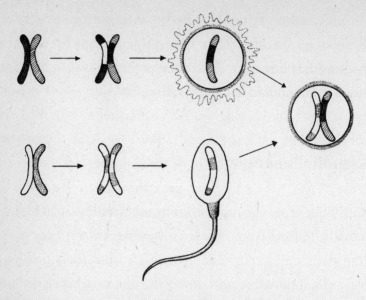

*Each half of each parent's chromosome comes from their own
parents. As a result of "crossing over," when each chromosome
is split again and brought together in parents' sperm and egg,
the baby will have genes from all four grandparents.*

covered DNA's shape. They proposed that genes are made
up of a double-stranded thread of millions of nucleic
acids. Just as the order of letters spells out words, the way
that these nucleic acids—life's alphabet—are strung together in the DNA spells out instructions for making life's
critical machinery, proteins. So sections of the string of
DNA, the bits of instructions for making individual proteins, are genes.

Each person has two complete sets of genes, one from each parent. In the process of making sperm and egg, the maternal strands of DNA and the paternal strands break at prearranged points and "cross over," mixing up the maternal and paternal genes on each resulting strand. This is why children not only have one set of genes from their mother and one from their father but also a selection of genes from each of the four grandparents. If this mixing didn't occur, the genes of one grandparent on each side would be tossed away during reproduction.

When genes are switched and mixed, the form and function of development proteins "coded" by these genes are changed. These changes are able to alter the shape of the body, the layout of the brain, and personality factors.

Double Trouble

Twins who have been separated at birth are the golden coins of the realm for human genetic analyses, because it is through them that researchers can attempt to differentiate the effects of nature versus nurture. Scientists can study these twins by following a classic scientific model: start with identical objects, place them in different environments, and test the difference the environment makes. In identical (or mono-ovular) twins, researchers have two people who possess exactly the same genes, because the twins came from the same fertilized egg. When scientists test identical twins separated at birth (usually through adoption) and raised apart, they are able to pick apart the usually hopelessly intertwined and tangled effects of genes and the environment. To make data more reliable, researchers compare these results with that of identical twins raised together and fraternal twins (who come from two different eggs and sperm and therefore have only as many genes in common as any siblings would) raised either apart or together.

Given the importance of twins in genetic research, it's fitting that one of the most recent, comprehensive studies of the genetic influences on behavior is taking place in the Twin Cities, at the University of Minnesota in Minneapolis–St. Paul. Since the 1970s, the scientists have studied hundreds of pairs of twins, over a hundred of which are identical. Through multiple exams that included thousands of questions, the researchers found that identical twins who are raised apart are just as likely to be similar in personality, temperament, occupational interests, leisure-time interests, and social attitudes as identical twins who are raised together. After crunching the statistical harvest from their exams through computers, the researchers came to the conclusion that, in general, genes contribute fully half of the influence on how we feel, how we think, and how we act.

What's more, although some personality traits were affected by environment more than by genes, for other traits genes were the dominant factor. The traits most affected by genes in this study (dubbed the "Minnesota Twins Study") were termed "social dominance" (the tendency to take the lead in groups) and traditionalism (high respect for rules, authority, and strict moral standards), which were found to be about 60 percent genetically determined. Other factors that were deemed mostly genetic were the ability to handle stress, dedication to hard work, and the ability to become rapt or engrossed during an experience.

In the process of locating and questioning identical twins who were raised apart, the scientists at the University of Minnesota came upon a remarkable number of eerie coincidences. There were two brothers who, though they were unaware of each other's existence, followed strangely parallel lives: each became a firefighter and each drank the same brand of beer while holding it with his little finger positioned under the can. The prize for "Twins Raised in Most Different Environments" could go to twins named Oskar and Jack. The first was raised in a Nazi family in Czechoslovakia, while the other was raised as a Jew on the Caribbean island of Trinidad. After being reunited, they discovered they shared a number of unusual habits, such as flushing the toilet before as well as after using it and enjoying startling people by sneezing loudly in elevators. Of course, such parallels, though interesting, are only sidelights of the study. The evidence for genetic influence on personality lies in the hundreds of thousands of bits of data from all the twins, not in just a few interesting coincidences.

The Minnesota Twins Study was not alone in finding that genes insert themselves strongly into personality. The Minnesota study distinguished itself by using a large number of twins who had been separated early in life, but other studies have come up with similar results by comparing identical twins with fraternal twins or other close relatives. One researcher, H. Hill Goldsmith of the University of Wisconsin–Madison, looked at temperaments in infants, at an age before most environmental effects have an influence. Goldsmith found that, in infants, the greatest personality differences between identical twins and fraternal twins (and therefore the areas of greatest genetic influence) were tendencies to be fearful, angry, or highly active. The lowest difference between infant twins (and therefore the least genetically influenced) was the ability to be soothed. Goldsmith knew that there is always the possibility that, even at such a young age, identical twins and fraternal twins might be treated differently. Knowing also that this might skew the results, Goldsmith was able to come up with a test that goes a long way toward removing that concern. Among the families he studied there were ten infant pairs whose parents thought they were fraternal twins, but on closer examination Goldsmith discovered they were identical. As expected—if Goldsmith's results are valid—the misidentified pairs fit the pattern of identical twins more closely than fraternal twins.

The phenomenon of misidentified twins brings up an interesting point, one that has some relevance in the nature-nurture debate. The point is that "identical" twins really never are. Twins can be identical genetically, but the decisions that cells and tissues make as they are developing aren't entirely governed by genes. There is a significant element of chance that goes into the process. Twins can even affect each other's development, and when they share the same placenta (as identical twins often do) there can be a serious struggle for nutrition between them. When born, one twin can be much smaller than the other because he has been muscled out of the soup line by his sibling rival. Usually the size difference disappears in the first few years, but other differences can remain. In fact, identical twins can look quite different all their lives. A number of twins involved in studies of Alzheimer's disease, twins whose height and features were markedly different and who seemed clearly fraternal, found out they were identical only when blood tests were taken as part of the study. Thus the parents' misidentification of their identical twins in Goldsmith's study is not as strange as it may seem at first.

Even identical twins that truly look identical have slight differences. The inherent differences among identical twins point up an extra factor usually not considered in nature-nurture discussions: the effect of developmental luck. Like the steel ball released at the top of a pachinko machine, cells in a developing baby may take one of a number of paths as a result of nothing more than chance. These random changes are independent of genes and what we usually think of as environmental factors.

The latest twist in the nature-nurture debate is that some of what seems to be nurture may in fact be nature. Some scientific researchers observe that, to some extent, people make their own environment based on their genetic predispositions. Genes that promote gregariousness will make someone inclined to seek out other people, which will reinforce sociability. Genes that promote a tendency toward solitary contemplation will lead someone to isolated spots, and perhaps give him less opportunity to practice social skills than he otherwise would.

The opposite side of the coin is that some genes seem to "turn on" only under some conditions or in some environments. Environment can affect how genes act. Some birds aren't merely genetically programmed to sing their songs. The genes that allow them to learn the songs are "turned on" only when they hear a certain song from birds of the same species. If they don't hear the species song they never sing it right. The correct song hits an inborn cord; it resonates within the genes.

Caution: Genetic Construction Ahead

Scientists who conduct genetic research on behavior make a number of warnings. Most important, genetic effects on personality traits can never be totally dominant. Personality and intelligence are always affected by environment and upbringing. In addition, there are likely many genes that influence personality; each gene probably has a small effect. Therefore, no one is likely ever to isolate the "popularity gene." Even claims that scientists have found single genes for individual diseases or addictions, such as depression and alcoholism, have not held up to scientific scrutiny. Such claims have often been made and retracted, and there are still no single gene candidates for any widespread psychological disorder.

Yet the more precise and careful nature of recent genetics work has begun to win over those skeptical of behavioral genetics. Whereas even fifteen or twenty years ago it was anathema to suggest that genes have a significant effect on behavior, the idea has now become fairly well accepted. Even a genetic influence on intelligence, which was once taboo to proclaim, is now widely asserted to lie between 30 percent and 70 percent. Many scientists who previously opposed such research have begun to agree with much of it, even as they continue to voice concerns about the application of the information.

Other scientists continue to oppose behavioral genetics, seeing it as an irresponsible continuation of past shoddy science. They see the studies as inherently opposed to attempts at social reform. Many behaviorial geneticists counter that their research actually sets the stage for social reforms that work better. If people are treated as individuals, with individual genetic strengths and weaknesses, they say, then reform efforts can be tailored to their needs.

More Genes: Function to Form

The other major area of genetic research that has begun to crack open in the last decade is the study of how genes shape our bodies. This research constitutes one of the great movements of modern biology, and no book on what scientists know about how babies develop would be complete without it. The research addresses not simply the question of how a thin or a fat nose is passed down from generation to generation. What scientists are puzzling over is more general—not only why we look different from each other, but why we look different from other animals. Scientists are in the process of discovering the very blueprints that define how we are built and the workings of the evolutionary architects that mold all animals through time.

Nobel Laureate Gerald Edelman, a professor of neuroscience at the University of California, San Diego, compares studying development to watching a stage play. You can see the stage and the curtains. You watch the sets change and the actors spin out their lines. But if you want to understand how the theater functions, you need to get backstage and inspect the electrical and mechanical works that make it all possible. "We're now beginning to see the guy wires backstage that make everything go," Edelman says.

Boxed Set

In the last chapter we learned that biologists are coming to understand how a single cell can grow into a layer of cells, and how that layer can fold, stretch, and change to form a body, a face, and limbs. But many other animals have a body, face, and limbs. Why don't all these animals look alike? And why don't we look like each other?

The common answer to all these questions is that the difference is in the genes. But what genes are these? What is happening backstage to let the show go forward, time after time, generation after generation?

Scientists have been puzzling out that basic question for over a century, and making good progress in the last few decades. In the 1980s there was a major leap forward, though, when scientists began applying the techniques of genetic engineering to the problem on a wide scale. Not only did the researchers start to find the ways genes drive the behavior of cells, they were also shocked and delighted to find an incredible kinship among all animals, from man to fly, from mouse to the microscopic wisp of a worm called *C. elegans.* They discovered that even though these other animals look nothing like us, the master genes that determine their body shape are very similar to ours. In fact, not only are we cut from the same cloth, but nature uses the same shears. This recognition has spawned one of the most interesting and productive expeditions ever on the frontiers of biology, a search for the genes that support and tie together all the rungs of the evolutionary ladder.

A major part of the story of this discovery begins at the University of Basel in Switzerland. As with many of the most important genetic discoveries of this century, the subject of the research at the university was not human beings or even mice: it was *Drosophila melanogaster,* the lowly fruit fly. A European scientist named Walter Gehring was searching for the master genes of development in the flies: genes that sit at the top of the developmental heap, controlling other genes. In the early 1980s, Gehring was studying the gene for a very peculiar mutation, one that kept flies from developing antennae. Instead, where the antennae should be, the flies grew legs. The gene, called *antennapedia* (Latin for antenna-feet), seemed to be just one such master gene, a gene that turned on many others, thereby switching a whole group of cells from one function to another. In the spring of 1983, Gehring's researchers triumphantly isolated a stretch of DNA that belonged to this gene.

In one of those strange examples of scientific synchronicity, at the time Gehring's colleagues were isolating part of the *antennapedia* gene, a quarter of the way around the world in a laboratory at Indiana University, a young post-doctoral student named Matthew Scott isolated virtually the same gene fragment through an entirely different line of investigation.

What was particularly interesting about the *antennapedia* gene was that it contained a key sequence of the genetic code, the ordering of the four nucleotide letters—abbreviated A, T, C, and G—that spell out the language of heredity. When comparing the sequences of different gene codes, it's common practice to highlight similarities between the genes by drawing a box around the common sequences, like this:

. . . GCTTATCCACATACGA⬚TATAGG⬚CACTATAGTCGTAG . . .

. . . CACTCTTTTGCTCCTGG⬚TATAGG⬚TCCTAAAGCGCCATT. . .

The scientists in Gehring's lab saw how the 180-letter se-quence from *antennapedia* kept popping up in many other genes. Were these the master developmental genes? Since students could isolate, or box, the common sequence and the genes were a type called homeotic, they called the se-quence a homeobox.

What happened next provided the first evidence that these genes were not just important to fruit flies. In the laboratory next to Gehring's was another scientist, Eddy De Robertis. De Robertis, now a professor of biological chemistry at the University of California, Los Angeles, was also looking for the master genes of development, but in an entirely different organism, the fat South African clawed frog, *Xenopus laevus*. When De Robertis heard of Gehring's triumph he decided he wanted to look for homeobox genes in frogs.

De Robertis's search was easier than Gehring's: by using Gehring's DNA as a molecular lure, he could go "fishing" in the frog DNA for any homeobox genes. When De Robertis dipped Gehring's lure into the frog's gene pool, he quickly got three bites—three genes containing homeoboxes that were almost identical to those in the fly. De Robertis broke out the champagne.

Since then, scientists have gone on what Harvard

biologist Stephen Jay Gould calls one of the most productive fishing trips in history, pulling out homeobox-containing genes from many species, including chickens, mice, birds, worms, and humans. It is likely these genes provide the forces that mold us, shape the embryo, and guide the changes that were outlined in the last chapter. How these genes work, and their relation to each other, shines an intriguing bit of light on nature's fascinating plan. Perhaps the best way to explain is to use a musical analogy.

Variations on a Theme

Beethoven's *Symphony No. 5 in C minor, Opus 67,* begins with a simple, direct, and dramatic series of four notes. *Da-da-da-daaaah.* These four notes have become so famous that Beethoven's name is immediately associated with them. They are the notes that Beethoven himself thought of as "fate knocking at the door." They became the morse-coded "V for Victory" for the Allies during World War II. They have become so well known, and the symphony itself has become so overplayed, that people lose sight of the reason that the symphony, especially its first movement, is considered among the greatest of musical masterpieces.

The first four notes of the first movement are dramatic,

but what comes after them sets it apart. Quite simply, Beethoven bases the whole movement on the pattern of that simple quartet of notes. After the first four notes there is a pause, and the orchestra repeats the four notes shifted down a whole tone. Then the violins take up the theme, stating the quadruplet and building on it, repeating it, changing it. Other instruments come in and make their own modifications to the theme. They offer a counterpoint to the theme, then a harmony, then a dynamic give and take—until the whole orchestra is engaged in a driving, complex hallelujah based on the initial few notes. Beethoven's audacious goal in the first movement of his fifth symphony was to produce diversity from unity.

The genetic performance that produces a human being from a fertilized egg plays out along the same principle: from one to many. From simplicity to complexity. What begins with the action of a few genes becomes a harmonic crescendo of thousands acting in concert. These genes form a kind of chain letter, a molecular phone tree. As the cells divide, one gene makes proteins that turn on many more genes that, in turn, do the same to others. By the time a child is born, the body's 100,000 genes form an elaborate mosaic, some bursting with activity, others silently awaiting their marching orders.

Which genes play the basic theme in shaping the body? The homeobox genes have been good candidates.

For one thing, many of them are known to be critical in determining body structures and shape. For another, the proteins produced by genes with the homeobox sequence have the perfect shape to insert themselves into DNA's twisted double helix, fitting like a key inside a lock. Recently, however, the homeobox genes were discovered to be subservient to a more primary set of genes named "hedgehog" genes. Scientists think that hedgehog may be the primary shapemaker genes.

The homeobox and hedgehog genes act like an identification code, says Matthew Scott, the post-doc who helped discover the homeobox genes. Scott, now a professor at Stanford University, compares the genes to a tree identification book. "These books ask, 'Does it have leaves or needles? Do the leaves have knobs? Are the leaves flat?' " says Scott. The reader narrows down his choices by answering these questions, eventually arriving at an exact identity for the tree. Similarly, the homeobox and hedgehog genes act as a book that determines each cell type through a series of yes or no answers, then sets in motion the machinery that makes the cell behave a certain way. Learning to manipulate these genes may eventually help us regenerate cells or repair tissues.

Distant Echoes

The fact that the homeobox genes in fruit flies, mice, and humans are so similar helps explain an old observation. In the late nineteenth century, Ernst Haekel noted that early embryos of many creatures look astoundingly alike. In fact, when he forgot to label samples of embryos from different species, he couldn't tell which was which. In voluminous writings, Haekel popularized an explanation for this phenomenon in a phrase: "Ontogeny recapitulates phylogeny"—which is to say, development is a review of evolution. Modern biologists have rejected this notion because Haekel's idea was that at each state in the development of a human baby, the embryo actually takes the form of an *adult* animal in evolutionary development. Haekel thought that a baby first *became* a worm, then a fish with gills, then an amphibian with webbed limbs, and so on. If some of these stages looked like no living animal, Haekel thought, then the animal represented must just be extinct.

Like all good myths, Haekel's idea contains a grain of truth. The truth in it is that development does have some aspects of our evolutionary past. All vertebrates start out using a similar set of homeobox genes to get their shape. Humans start out looking like the fish embryos, complete with the slits that fish will eventually make into gills, but then we take a different path. The slits that become gills in

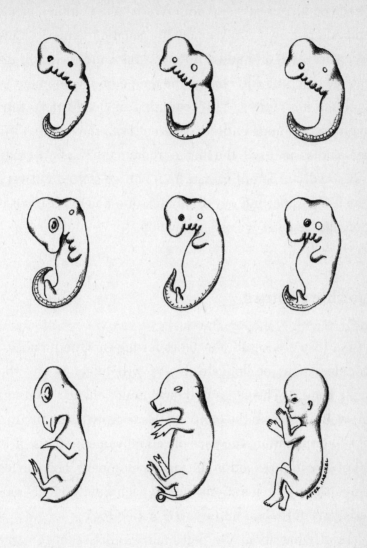

fish become our ears and chin. We take the old fish genes and add our own riff. We take the genetic themes in mice (or even yeast) and add a little jazz here and there, duplicate gene motifs and change the tempo of development to produce new forms. The beginning of Beethoven's fifth symphony sounds entirely different from the end, but the same notes are used, the themes remain the same. We may look totally different from a frog, but we started out very much the same, and our differences are due to improvisation on the genes we use to develop.

Double Feature

When they are found, the genes for jug ears, petite noses, hopeless hair, or delicate fingers will likely follow the same pattern. The genes will have minor changes that improvise slightly on the tempo of tissue growth, the rhythm of cell duplication, the pace of cell movements. This little bit of jazz improvisation during development then carries down through generations, giving each family its characteristic features and cultures a common look.

And what about the personalities that seem to carry down through the generations? How do the genes for behavior fit into this pattern? As observed before, any given personality characteristic is likely the result of many genes, so isolating these genes may be difficult or impossible in the near future. But if they ever are isolated, they probably will follow suit with the genes for body form. Genes that contribute to personality might create a small bulge in one area of the brain, like genes for a bulbous nose create a swelling on the tip of the proboscis. They might make one kind of nerve cell especially active, or make a population of nerve cells grow out more aggressively. In determining behavior, genes seem to set the questions that are answered in the growing brain.

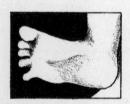

actual size

THE FIFTH MONTH

(Weeks 18–21 after conception;
weeks 20–23 after LMP)

During this month the fetus makes a major change in appearance. The sebaceous glands, the oil-producing organs that will cause so much complexion trouble in adolescence, begin working. The sebum that these glands produce and dead skin cells accumulate in a white, cheesy coating all over the baby's body. This slather, called the vernix caseosa, protects the baby from skin problems that can result from sitting too long in his warm bath. By the end of this month, the baby is completely covered with fine hairs (lanugo), which may help the vernix caseosa stick to the skin.

During this month most mothers will certainly feel the fetus move. When she begins to feel the first movement it is commonly called the quickening. By the end of the month, the fetus begins to acquire a regular schedule of sleeping and kicking. He also gets the protection of his own primitive immune system, which is able to protect him against some infections.

The middle of this month is the mid-point of pregnancy, and the fetus is about half of the 50 centimeters (20 inches) that babies measure in total length (on average) upon delivery. By the end of the month, the fetus is 30 centimeters (12 inches) from head to heel, and curled into a packet 20 centimeters (8 inches) across. His weight has lagged behind his length, though, because at this point he still weighs less than 500 grams (about a pound), one-seventh the average delivery weight. From this point on, the baby will start putting on weight quickly, even as the lengthening process slows down.

FIVE

THE THOUGHT MACHINE

WHEN YOU WATCH CHILDREN ONE OR TWO YEARS OLD, when you slow down to their pace and get down to their level, it is easy to marvel at how they soak up the world around them and learn to manipulate it (and the people around them). Kids this age are learning the everyday physics of things dropping and pounding, and magnets sticking, and hooks hooking. They are beginning to actively play with other children rather than just play next to them, inventing among themselves a mini-society. They are expressing will, and throwing tantrums, and finding humor in the world around them. And they are deciphering the meanings of words and learning to create the sounds that represent objects and actions.

To watch their young minds form is to wonder at the brain itself. This two-pound mass of tissue is the seat of each personality and the font of their creativity. It drives their curiosity and is molded by their learning. It is the interpreter of the world around them, but is still imperfect—a twisted funhouse mirror that reflects and distorts experience.

The formation of the brain is perhaps the most incredible part of the journey from cell to self. Something magical happens in the growing baby to endow her with a structure far more advanced than any computer ever built, far more subtle and complex than any other known object in the universe.

What happens to the brain as it blossoms in the womb? How is it possible that the unknowing embryo can build a complex reservoir for knowledge? Why are some kids smarter than others? How is it that some become writers or painters, while others develop a talent for numbers or for mechanical devices?

Scientists are searching for answers about how the brain works and how nature manufactures this marvelous structure. And they are succeeding—we have learned more about the brain in the last ten years than in all of previous history.

The story researchers are piecing together about how the brain develops is fascinating. It is the story of voyager neurons that move across the vast sweep of the brain to find a home, pioneers that search out paths for others to follow. It is the story of how families of neurons follow their fates generation after generation, and how tens of thousands of nerve cells die off in a massive suicide that is necessary for the brain to function properly. But how the unimaginably complex whole forms itself is not just an interesting story in itself. Many scientists now think that knowledge about the mechanics of brain development holds answers to ancient questions. Knowledge about how nerve cells in the body and brain learn to function may tell us what consciousness is and where it is located in the brain, what memories are made of, and what goes wrong in mental illness.

Scientists are already trying to use the information to build more powerful computers that think a little less like their rigid and literal predecessors and a little more like humans. Our emerging understanding of the brain may also tell us how we form ideas about the world, perceive, and remember.

Most intriguing of all, new knowledge about the brain gives us a peek into the experience of life in the womb.

Although the process of coming into being, of acquiring consciousness, will always be alien to us who have left it behind, we may still be able to empathize with some of the baby's experiences in utero. With the help of science, we may be able to know a few of the things that are going through babies' minds as they grow and become during their long half-slumber in the womb. Because there is something going on in their minds, something both strange and very familiar.

To Sleep, Perchance to Dream

During the last four to six weeks of pregnancy, the expectant mother finds it more difficult than ever to sleep as the medicine ball attached to her midsection presses in and stretches out. Some may find it galling that during this time the fetus spends about 95 percent of her time asleep. Some mothers may say this is not possible, that one of the *reasons* they can't sleep is that the kung fu artist inside is keeping them up most of the night. But the baby's kicking and jabbing are just actions of a poor bedmate. These muscular movements occur mostly during light sleep, just the way anyone might roll over or move a leg in the middle of the night.

Most of the baby's time asleep is spent in deep sleep,

when she doesn't move her limbs much at all. However, when the fetus falls into this deep sleep, something begins to happen. Her eyes flutter. Her pulse increases. Her muscles twitch subtly. Inside the brain there are more dramatic goings-on: a cluster of nerves deep in the brain stem initiates an explosion of neural activity that bolts throughout the brain. Oxygen consumption in the brain increases. Electromagnetic messages zing back and forth across the cranium, through cell clusters and nerve nets. If the fetus were hooked up to a machine that measures brain activity, the indicator needle would jerk wildly.

If this sounds familiar, it should: it happens to you every night. About ninety minutes after you fall asleep, you enter a period of rapid eye movement (REM) sleep. Your breathing and heart rates increase, your muscles twitch. And later, whether you remember it or not, you dream. REM sleep and the accompanying dreams will repeat every ninety minutes or so. Most people get about two hours of REM sleep during eight hours of sleep.

By all measurable indicators, REM in the fetus seems to be almost identical to REM in adults. During REM sleep in the womb, babies have the same rapid eye movements, pulse changes, and muscle twitches. And they have a major increase in brain activity and brain metabolism. So the question becomes: do babies also dream in the womb? Do they also tune into the midnight show on Channel 1, the sometimes scary, sometimes comforting mélange of feelings and impressions we know so well?

The baby can't have visual dreams; he doesn't yet have visual experience, and his visual cortex in the brain is still undeveloped. But this doesn't preclude dreaming. Although we tend to think of dreams primarily as an interweaving of visual images, blind people dream too, of sounds and feelings. Dreaming is mainly visual for most of us because we are mostly visual creatures. If one's daily experiences and thoughts consist of touch or sounds, then the dreams will be woven from that cloth. Chefs are said to dream, in exquisite detail, of the flavors and aromas of food. Dreams are daily experiences that are swept up in the night-stream of the rushing mind.

With this in mind, we can infer that babies do have dreams of a sort. After all, every measurable sign of REM sleep is the same in the child as it is in the mother. The child can hear, feel, and otherwise sense his surroundings. He can even consolidate those sensations enough to form an extremely simple memory of them. We can never be certain that the fetus dreams, because we can never ask him, but we can guess that he does.

Of course, the dreams of the mother and child would not be alike. The dreams of the fetus would likely be woven from the simple sensations of the world around him. It is easy to imagine that the sleeping child waiting to be born dreams a kaleidoscopic pastiche of the day's events: voices, the beat of the mother's heart, the squeeze of the womb, the sway of the pelvis, the pulse of the jack-hammer the mother passed on the street.

An Active Mind

In the last trimester of pregnancy, the baby's sleep is far from empty. A symphony of nerve activity is playing inside his tiny cranium. The ensemble of millions of nerve signals creates a constant ebb and flow of brain waves. Electrochemical shots are firing to and fro, even as the brain is growing.

What is the purpose of all this brain activity before birth? Scientists have long suspected that it must be doing something. After all, the biggest measurable difference between REM in the fetus and REM in adults is that the fetus spends a lot more time at it. "During the last month in the womb, the fetus spends about 60 percent of its sleep time in REM sleep," explains Dr. Bryan Richardson, who studies fetal REM at St. Joseph's Health Care Centre in London, Ontario. "That would suggest an important role for REM" before birth.

Scientists have long speculated that the brain's activity in the womb is part of the process of brain development. Now the evidence of modern neuroscience is beginning to support that idea and form a picture of the growing brain. The brain is molded by a combination of genetic nature and environmental nurture, a mix of careful planning and chance. Genetic instructions create a framework for thought, but the ultimate directions that nerves receive for wiring the brain are like those in an old joke: When a visitor to New York City asks a native how to get to Carnegie Hall, the New Yorker responds, "Practice, practice, practice."

The genetic instruction to the developing brain produces an overabundance of nerve tissue, a teeming neurological tangle that has too many brain cells and too many connections between them. The brain is active before birth because it is the nerve activity, the practice, that disciplines the tangled mess of nerves into workable wiring.

But before the brain can practice, it has to make the players, move them into position, and link them up to each other.

The Budding Brain

The basic working units of the brain are the neurons. These cells send messages to each other across narrow gaps between the cells called synapses. They gather these messages through a branched fan of extensions called axons.

Neural cells first appear in the top layer of the three-level cake of the very early embryonic disc. The disc's top layer, the one next to the amniotic sac, eventually becomes the skin and nerves; the other two layers become everything else in the body. It is fitting that skin cells and nerve cells are born of the same exclusive stock. After all, skin is the boundary between ourselves and the outside world. Skin cells are the outpost on the frontier, the cells that come in direct contact with pressure, touch, warmth, and cold. Skin cells keep the world out. The nerves are like skin cells that have been internalized and specialized for a different purpose—they sense the outside world and bring it in. They are the messengers that carry back news from the frontier and make it part of us.

During the third week of development, the top layer of cells folds over on itself and forms a U-shaped culvert. At the beginning of the fourth week, it is roofed over to form a tube. The closing of the tube starts at the center of the disk and moves toward the ends, as if two zipper slides are moving away from each other. In the walls of this tube are about 125,000 cells, about the same number as there are people in two packed football stadiums. From these cells will grow every nerve cell in the brain and spinal cord, which, by the time of birth, will number 100 billion (about 20 times Earth's population). The front third of the tube becomes the brain; the rest becomes the spinal cord.

At first the tube is pretty straight, but even by the end of the third week it is beginning to bulge in spots that grow faster than others. The brain is also growing so much faster than the head of the embryo that by the fourth week it starts to bend and fold over on itself. By the fourth and fifth weeks, the part of the brain that will become the eyes is already reaching out for the surface of the nascent face, and at the tip of the new brain are two small buds. These tiny buds will eventually become the two cerebral hemispheres, the largest and most visible parts of the brain and the place where all higher thought takes place. By the seventh week of development, the cerebral hemispheres have grown as large as the rest of the brain and have coiled back over it. Soon the cerebral hemispheres are reversing direction in growth again, coiling around and growing forward to become the temporal (behind the temple) lobes. At this point the cerebral hemispheres have become so big that they cover the rest of the brain like a helmet.

The Incredible Journey

On a microscopic level, brain cells are making vast rearrangements and sweeping changes. The brain grows not just by multiplying its cells but also by moving cells around. Even in the first trimester, nerve cells are journeying from the center of the brain to its outer edge and from one end to the other. Interference with the migration of cells into

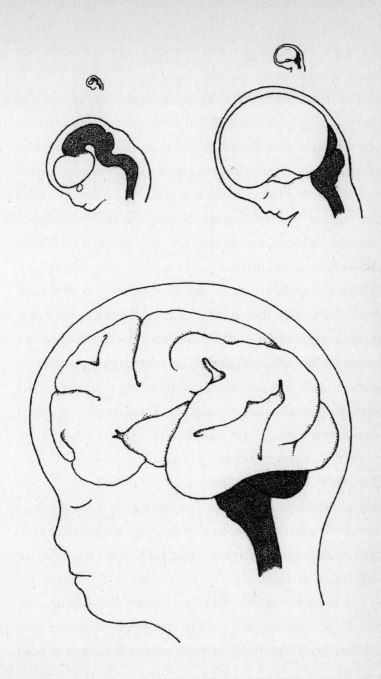

new regions during prenatal development can have dire consequences.

The most important of these regions is the cortex, the thin rind of gray matter that sheaths the cerebral hemispheres. (The word *cortex* comes from the Greek word for tree bark; *cork*—made from the bark of oak trees—traces to the same root.) Once built, the cortex will be the place where most information processing in the brain takes place. In children and adults, it is the home of all higher intellectual functioning.

Cortical cells are born in cell nurseries deep in the brain. From there they travel the great distance to the cortex with a snail-like motion, reaching out along wire-like support cells called glia, grabbing, and pulling themselves forward. And like the waves of pioneers that settled the West, each new batch of cells from the nurseries travels through the part of the cortex that has already been settled to establish a new community, a new layer of cells, beyond them. How these layers become established is very important, and scientists are discovering that if cells stumble along their path to the cortex, if the cells get stuck or confused, the result can be cognitive problems or mental illness in later life.

An example of this was discovered in Scandinavia. Finnish scientists, using their country's extensive and detailed health records, were studying how and whom schizophrenia struck. This terrible mental illness is typified by withdrawal from others, hallucinations, and disordered thoughts and behavior. The Finnish researchers looked at the medical records of schizophrenics and their families for clues to the cause of the disease and found a higher incidence of schizophrenia among those whose mothers had contracted influenza during the second trimester of pregnancy. The second trimester of pregnancy also happens to be when certain key nerve cells are migrating to the cortex. When scientists look for some of these key cells in schizophrenic brains, they find that cells have moved to the area just below the cortex, but don't seem to have made it in. Their hypothesis is that the influenza virus interferes with cell communication during the cell migration, perhaps hindering the cell's movements or tampering with the signposts that guide them.

This does not mean that any mother who gets the flu in the second trimester is going to have a schizophrenic child. The chances that any child will be schizophrenic are small, and flu during the second trimester of pregnancy raises the total odds of such an occurrence just slightly.

Thinning the Garden

Having lots of brain cells that make lots of connections doesn't necessarily make someone smarter. In fact, certain cognitive problems are associated with having too many cells in certain regions of the brain. The explanation for this apparent paradox is the role of practice in brain development.

Like recent college graduates, new neurons network like crazy in hopes of finding a job. They shoot out a fan of tendrils in order to make links with nearby cells. They dispatch vine-like axons that follow the trail of their desires to distant brain regions. The growing axons are fitted with sensitive tips called growth cones that reach out and connect to other cell surfaces. The growth cones are programmed to like some surfaces and to shrink away from others. The growing axons also follow their nose, wiggling into streams of free-floating chemicals to link up with the cells that are releasing them. Once neurons connect with other cells and form synapses, they start exchanging electrochemical messages.

Not every cell finds a place in the organization, however. Those neurons that can't find a useful job are eliminated. Or rather, they do themselves in, blowing out their cell walls and pulverizing their DNA. By the time the culling is all over, fully half of the approximately 200 billion neurons that exist at the peak of their population will have been wiped out. And what happens if some of the cells that should die do not? In 1991, scientists found that this overpopulation could be at the root of some kinds of dyslexia.

For people with dyslexia, reading is an arduous chore. Those with dyslexia can identify letters but don't recognize the words they form, perhaps as a result of a mistiming of nerve signals. When people with dyslexia see a word, they recognize it as a word, but it doesn't "speak" to them; it doesn't instantly call up a picture.

Sometimes, when those with dyslexia read a sentence very slowly, carefully sounding out each letter, the meaning of the words will click for them. Although many teachers mistakenly think dyslexic students are simply not bright, the disorder has nothing to do with intelligence or lack of it. Some very bright people in history, including Thomas Edison, are thought to have been dyslexic, and people with the disorder have successfully completed law and medical schools.

Michael Duara of the University of Miami School of Medicine in Florida used magnetic resonance imaging (MRI) to look at the size of a certain area of the cortex that lies in the rear of the brain, near the groove that splits the two hemispheres. In most people, this area is smaller on the right side of the brain than it is on the left. What Duara found was that in those with dyslexia the situation is reversed. That area on the right side of the brain is bigger, or the same size, as on the left. What's more, the corpus callosum—the band of fibers connecting the two halves of the brain—is larger in those with dyslexia. Duara and his colleagues theorize that the excess brain cells in these areas are tied up with the cause of dyslexia. They also speculate that the surfeit of cells could be due to an error during development that allowed some cells marked for death to live.

Cells That Fire Together, Wire Together

In addition to killing excess cells, the brain generates a densely woven snarl of the nerve connections, and then prunes back the excess. The number of connections involved is nearly unimaginable. Each of the 100 billion nerve cells in the brain is able to make thousands of connections. Some cells make 200,000 connections each. So the estimated number of connections in the brain is astronomical. University of Chicago professor Peter Huttenlocher has made a survey of the actual number of neural connections in people at different ages and found that, when the fetus is twenty-four weeks old, the 70,000 cells in a piece of brain tissue the size of a pinhead make about 124 million connections.

How does the brain decide which connections should stay and which should go? How does the brain decide which ones are good and which are bad? Again, the answer probably lies in practice.

The process of sending signals zinging through zillions of connections in itself tests the brain circuits and begins to allow bits of the brain to form tiny functional units. Use shapes the connections in the brain just like use shapes a road system: old, unused roads are let go and may eventually be reclaimed by the wilderness around them. Well-used roads are built up and improved. In the developing brain, nerve connections that are used are strengthened; those that are not are eliminated or weakened.

What's more, certain *patterns* of use strengthen nerve connections. When two signals arrive at a cell at the same time, the connections that brought those signals in are selectively strengthened. The pathways that bring in random signals are ignored. This allows nerve cells to sort out the signals and circuits that are meaningful.

One example of the way it seems to work is this: When the fetus kicks his foot against the inside of his mother's belly, a group of sensory nerves in one spot of the foot simultaneously sends many signals to the brain. The signals follow different pathways, and they may flow to many different parts of the brain. But in one spot in the sensory cortex, the signals converge. The connections between cells that receive this simultaneous signal are strengthened, and

the connections between cells that receive random signals (from elsewhere in the brain or body) are weakened, or eliminated. What results is a spot on the brain that is committed to registering sensations from only that spot on the foot.

Other research has shown that often-used connections are even more receptive to further signaling, making them even stronger. Many researchers compare this process to Darwin's survival of the fittest, because neurons struggle to make the strongest connections and dominate others. Nobelist Gerald Edelman has even constructed a theory called "neural Darwinism," based on a competitive, evolutionary model of neural selection.

Modern neuroscience has made it clear that from early in pregnancy, the baby's brain is buzzing away because it must. Just as every cell requires oxygen, the brain requires activity to develop correctly. For more than any other part of the body, it is use and practice that shapes this organ, and forms the raw material from which future thoughts and emotions will be shaped in turn.

The primary role of brain activity in shaping the functions of the brain also begins to explain how this unimaginably complex device is created when the information contained in the body's roughly 100,000 genes isn't nearly enough to provide an explicit wiring diagram. The answer is that genes provide only a framework for development. The genetically programmed preferences of nerve cells sets limits on their multiplication and movement. The genes are the broad brush that sets down fields of color on the canvas of the brain. The electrochemical pointillism of brain activity will supply the details in the total picture of brain wiring. For this reason, the brains of identical twins aren't identical. Their genes may create many similarities in the general layout of their brains, but there is an element of chance in where neurons make connections and how they fire, and therefore the wiring of their brains before birth will be different.

If activity shapes the detailed wiring of the brain, then whatever affects neural activity in the developing brain should also affect brain construction. Early evidence from animal research is showing that in some cases even a pregnant mother's own thoughts and emotions may be able to make permanent changes in her baby's brain.

Stressed Bequest

In Ned Kalin's lab at the University of Wisconsin, the rats are pregnant and under a lot of stress. Kalin and his colleagues have found that the pregnant rats react to stress as all rats (and humans) do: their adrenaline levels rise and they shift their metabolism to ready energy for fight or flight. They also produce more of the hormones called glucocorticoids. These are steroid hormones that have been shown to change the way genes act. During long-term stress, the circulating stress hormones can change nerve wiring in the brain and make someone much more reactive to other stresses.

What Kalin has discovered is that the mother's stress affects not only her reactions but also those of her babies. And those effects continue on even after birth. Pups born to mothers under certain kinds of stress during the pregnancy were much more reactive to stress after birth, Kalin found, and were more hesitant about playing with others. What's more, the heightened reaction to stress persisted as they grew older.

Kalin surmises that the glucocorticoids, the stress hormones, are creating the edgy and irritable rat pups. The steroid hormones probably change the environment, the milieu, in which the developing neurons make their decisions. As the brain goes through its paces in the womb, the stress hormones probably affect how cells react to stimulation and give an edge to the selection of stress-related circuits. Once those circuits and stress connections are set up, they continue to function into adulthood.

Although the news is sobering, the research is still too new to know if it applies to humans. There is one bright spot, however. The mother's stress affected her offspring only when she had no control over how and when it was delivered. When the mother rat had some control over when the stress was administered, the pups turned out fine. "This suggests that we may be able to intervene to block the effects," Kalin says. "We might be able to teach people strategies to help them deal with stress better and to feel they have some control over it."

REM and Remembrance

Knowing what they know about the role of nerve activity in brain development, scientists may be able to solve the question that was touched on in the beginning of this chapter: the decades-old mystery of the primary purpose of REM. Since its discovery more than thirty years ago, scientists have proposed a number of theories about the use of REM sleep. They range from clearing the mind of interfering or useless thoughts to making memories stick, to keeping the brain warmed—the engine revved up—so the thoughts are ready to roll upon waking.

The first function of REM sleep, though, seems to be to create the protothoughts, feelings, and impressions that are the final act of rehearsal that creates the working brain. After initial nerve activity has established a bit of organization, the brain activity of REM sleep choreographs brain development on a larger scale. The brain-stem regions that initiate REM could in effect be manufacturing simulated thoughts and emotions through higher centers of the brain. Running these protothoughts through the brain could help supply the operating rules for later brain function.

This idea raises an interesting possibility. REM sleep might not be something that the fetus acquires because he is getting older and more like us. We might dream because when we sleep we are like fetuses. If REM sleep's primary purpose is to assist in brain development, our dreams could be the leftovers from that process (although REM sleep seems to have been adapted for other useful functions in adults). REM sleep and dreaming could be a kind of mental belly button, an artifact that serves as a daily reminder of where we came from.

Our need for REM sleep definitely declines as we get

older. From the 60 percent of sleep time spent in REM before birth, there is a steady decline until adolescence, when the fraction of sleep time taken up by REM has fallen to 20 to 25 percent. After that the decline is more gradual, dropping to 15 to 20 percent of total sleep in old age.

The phantasmagoria of strange characters and situations that run through the mind at night, then, could be just the collection of experiences that get in the way of the neural signals emanating from the brain stem as it carries out its old developmental program. One Japanese researcher goes so far as to say that dreaming is a reversion to a fetal state. Our own dreams might be a small window on fetal life, mirroring some of the strangeness that the fetus must experience as he inhabits the twilight world between conception and birth, between nothingness and being.

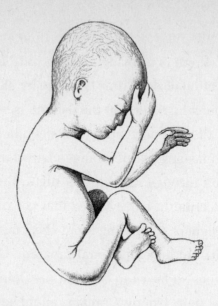

actual size

THE SIXTH MONTH

(Weeks 22–26 after conception;
weeks 24–28 after LMP)

This month marks a major transition. For the first time, the fetus is able to survive outside the womb, albeit with a lot of modern medical help. Week 22 marks the far twilight zone of fetal viability, and many premature babies do not survive outside the womb even with extensive help. But by the 24th week, the fetal lungs have just begun making surfactant—the detergent-like molecule that helps lungs expand and take in air. By the 26th week, the chances of a prematurely born baby surviving in a neonatal intensive care ward are greatly improved.

A sign of the maturing nervous system is that by the 24th week (26th week after LMP), half of all fetuses are startled by loud noises—but there is usually a noticeable gap between the sound and the response. By this time the fetus also starts remembering sounds, storing primitive memories of music he hears and the sounds of his mother's voice. In the 26th week (28th after LMP), the eyes open once again, and the fetus exhibits early signs of being awake. By the end of the month the fetus's brainwaves resemble those of the newborn.

During this month, the baby really begins to put on weight and gains almost 500 grams (slightly more than one pound), about as much as he gained in the whole first half of the pregnancy. The fetus begins to look old and wrinkled because he still has little fat underneath the skin to fill it out, and because the lower and upper layers of skin have different growth rates. By the end of the month he has grown to about 35 centimeters (15 inches), and with his legs curled up measures about 25 centimeters (10 inches) across.

SIX

LIZARDS, SNAILS, AND PUPPY DOG TAILS

CRASH! ACROSS THE LAND, THREE-YEAR-OLD BOYS BOUNCE off walls and chairs, trip over toys, and bound down hallways. They hammer furniture and wield every stick like a gun. They carry on a compulsive relationship with construction equipment. What is more, they threaten to weaken and undermine something dear to many parents: not just the house, but a cherished, core belief that sex roles are created by society.

Mothers and fathers who came of age during or after

the sexual revolution have been immersed in a roiling, bubbling melting pot of sexual egalitarianism. The societal heat has been on to break down restrictive gender roles and allow women and men to mix more freely. One of the flames that fueled this fire was the assertion that society, not biology, created boys who were rough-and-tumble and girls who were interested in dolls. People began to accept that social reinforcement created men who couldn't talk about feelings and girls who were uninterested in car engines. Anyone who questioned this doctrine could get burned.

People knew that they themselves would never be able to break out of sexist thinking completely, but with their own kids they would wipe out sexism before it began. Many parents thought they would start with their own little tabula rasa and write a future free of sexism.

Then they had children.

Crash! They found that children have a habit of destroying many of their preconceived ideas about parenthood and childhood. Kaboom! Some of the cherished missing in action turned out to be their ideas about girls and boys. Sure, they found, the boys can learn to sew, but they also just seem to be more interested in certain "boy" things. The girls also are able to learn and enjoy a lot of activities traditionally reserved for boys, but they also seem to have a marked inclination toward "girl" things.

The parents were confused. Is it biology, after all, that determines how their children act? Or are they, as parents, unable to live up to their own ideals? Perhaps they secretly enjoy and reinforce the "right" behaviors; perhaps they are afraid of raising a tomboy or a sissy.

During this critical and confusing era, scientists are chiming in with a large body of new research on how critical aspects of gender and sexuality are shaped before we are born. The problem is that the research, though fascinating, leaves things more confused than ever. For all those who thought they learned in biology class what made girls girls and boys boys, think again. According to the research, there is more to sexuality than X and Y chromosomes. The brain is a sex organ, and the distinction between male and female is sometimes blurred. Conservatives, feminists, and gay rights activists have even fallen out among themselves as to whether the research findings are good or bad. Science may soon undermine old concepts so much that people may nostalgically start wishing for the days when "girls were girls and men were men" or forlornly remembering the "right-on" slogans of the past ("The only difference between men and women is what's between their legs").

That's What Little Boys Are Made Of

What makes a boy a boy and a girl a girl seems straightforward at first. As has been pounded into you numerous times since your junior high school "family life" or biology class, girls have two X chromosomes and boys have an X and a Y chromosome. This genetic match or mismatch is what drives the developing embryo into one of two different paths. Females are historically considered the default sex: if left to their own devices, genes on the large X chromosome will form a girl.

When the X chromosome is paired with the Y, the genetic interlopers on the relatively puny Y chromosome alter development for their own ends: the proliferation of guys.*

What is it about the Y chromosome that makes it act as a gender bender, veering "normal" female development in an entirely new direction? Scientists have known for some time that the whole Y chromosome isn't needed to create a guy instead of a girl. In fact, in 1991 British scientists won an international race to discover the single gene, out of hundreds on the Y chromosome and 100,000 in the body, that knocks over the first of the biochemical dominoes involved in making a male. Although the gene, called

---

*In fruit flies the opposite is true: the flies are destined to become male unless certain genes are activated to make the fly female.

SRY (sex-related gene of the Y chromosome), was discovered and tested in mice, it appears to operate the same way in all mammals, including people. Although SRY is the critical gender gene, it isn't really a "Guy Gene." It doesn't, by itself, create the swelled muscles, inflated egos, and other features that some people consider secondary sexual characteristics of the classic guy. Instead the SRY gene probably acts like a general, conveying orders to other genes, which pass the orders on to others until hundreds of genes set billions of cells marching off to manliness.

Genetically, the embryo is male or female from the moment of conception. In males, the SRY gene is sending out its masculinizing message from the time the whole embryo consists of no more than two cells. But otherwise, there don't seem to be any internal differences between males and females until the seventh week of development.

Externally, the growing genitals look similar in males and females until the ninth week. In fact, girls and boys develop the characteristics of both sexes during the early weeks of development. We are so used to thinking of men and women as opposites, as having totally different plumbing and equipment, that it can be a shock to find out how much the same they start out. It can be an eye-opener to realize that men and women really have almost exactly the same sex organs, just rearranged into different shapes and tailored for different purposes.

The sex organs begin to take shape when the germ cells, the diaspora that constitute the foundation of all the embryonic child's future descendants, migrate from the edge of the yolk sac into the body of the embryo. There, between the fifth and seventh weeks of development, they take up residence in two newly formed organs called the primordial gonads. Leading past each gonad on the way to the groin are two tubes, the Müllerian duct and the Wolffian duct.

As mentioned earlier, if the fetus is male—its cells have Y chromosomes and the SRY gene—the generic gonads will start to transform themselves into testes by the eighth week. If the cells have no Y chromosome (if the embryo is female), the generic gonads will wait as long as the thirteenth week for the male genes to come a-wooing. If none come calling by then, they commit themselves to becoming ovaries.

In boys, the newly formed testes start sending out two important chemical signals. The first is the hormone testosterone. The second is the protein Müllerian inhibiting factor. Under the influence of these signals, the female Müllerian duct atrophies and nearly disappears, the Wolffian ducts wrap one end of themselves around the testes, and the testes themselves descend into the groin.

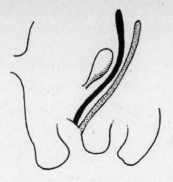

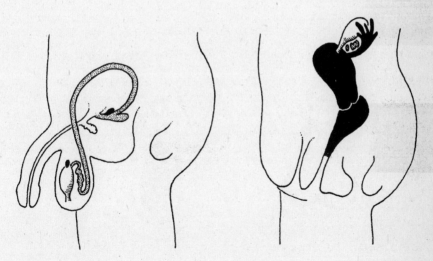

Both sexes start with both a Müllerian duct (black) and a Wolffian duct (gray). In girls the Müllerian duct becomes the female reproductive tract and the Wolffian duct dissolves. In boys the opposite occurs. Only a few scraps of the Müllerian duct remain near the testes and prostate.

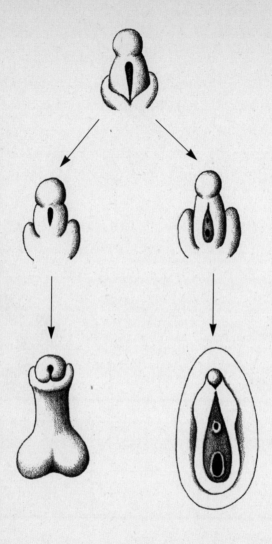

External sex organs also look the same at first. Different rates of growth in certain areas result in the formation of familiar male and female organs.

In girls, the absence of these signals cause the Wolffian duct to atrophy, and the Müllerian ducts reach out to the gonads (later to become the ovaries). The gonads stay up in the abdomen, and the Müllerian ducts become the fallopian tubes and the uterus.

What happens on the outside of the body is more dramatic retailoring of the same material. At about the sixth week, both boys and girls start with a tiny knob of flesh perched above a vertical slit of a membrane. The membrane will eventually dissolve and open a pathway to the bladder. Though this general genital area lacks definition, it looks more female than male. Without male hormones, the genitals become even more clearly female, as the knob of flesh becomes the clitoris and the vertical slit opens and is encircled by the labia minora and labia majora.

In boys, however, testosterone—and, more particularly, a cousin of testosterone called dihydrotestosterone (DHT)—shape these elements into something entirely different. The labia minora fuse and push forward to become the shaft of the penis, the fleshy knob becomes the hooded head of the penis, and the labia majora become sacs to contain the descended testes.

So it's all clear, right? The genetic combination of X and Y chromosomes decides whether the baby has ovaries or testes, and that determines whether the baby has a boy thing or a girl thing. Once X meets Y, it's a simple case of bing, bang, baby boy—right? Well, not necessarily. Gender confusion affects thousands of babies each year in the United States.

Some babies will grow up as one gender and then find themselves switching to the other. Other people will never question their gender identity until they are confronted with evidence that part of them belongs with the opposite sex. Consider the following stories:

Jenny

Jenny is a happy girl who has had a normal childhood. When she is twelve she waits for her period to begin. She is a little anxious when she doesn't start menstruating, but she knows that girls vary greatly in the rate at which they mature. By the age of fourteen she still hasn't started having her period, but something more shocking begins to happen. Her voice begins to drop, and hair begins to appear on her face. The right part of her groin, which has hurt for months, begins to swell visibly. Most frightening of all, her clitoris is growing and begins to resemble a penis. A trip to specialists reveals that she is genetically a boy, and that she will continue to develop more like a boy. After an initial period of shock, the family begins to adjust to the fact that their daughter is becoming a son, and start calling him John. But he is never really comfortable or accepted at school until he goes to college in another state.

Kelly

Kelly grew up in a small town in Ohio. Although she was always good-looking as a child, Kelly didn't become a striking beauty until adolescence. At that point, her perfect complexion, full breasts, slender limbs, and tall body made her the envy of other girls and filled the daydreams of the boys. When she turned seventeen she left school to start modeling for a well-known agency in New York City. She had several years of successful modeling, and when she was twenty-three she fell in love with and became engaged to an advertising executive.

Although she had never had a menstrual period, she refused to let it worry her. She chalked up the missed periods to the sports she played in high school and the strict diet and exercise she did to keep the near anorexic thinness of a model. But when she began to think about having children, she consulted a gynecologist. It shortly became apparent that Kelly had no ovaries and no uterus. Although this was extremely difficult for her to accept, it was not nearly as stunning as the reason: genetic tests revealed she was genetically male, but her body was not reacting to the male hormones called androgens. After much thought, she told her fiancé, who eventually came to accept the situation. They married and adopted children.

The stories above, although fictional, reveal common experiences for many people with these conditions. For instance, Kelly's condition, called androgen insensitivity syndrome, makes her better suited for modeling. Those with the syndrome tend to be tall, have long limbs, well-developed breasts, and clear skin. There have reportedly been a number of cases of androgen insensivity found among models.

Both Kelly and Jenny are genetically male, yet they lived at least part of their lives as girls. There are many other genetic conditions that yield equally confusing results. There are not only XY females, but also XX males, and true hermaphrodites who have both testicular and ovarian tissue. Are any of these *really* male or *really* female? To help answer that question, it helps to understand how the conditions in the two stories above came about.

In androgen insensitivity syndrome, the testes are formed normally and start producing testosterone, but the body doesn't react to this hormone and its associated antigens. When the body's cells don't recognize androgens, they take the feminine course of development. Externally, the body appears normal: female genitals appear, breasts develop at puberty and the voice stays high. But because the testes are also making the Müllerian inhibiting factor, the interior parts of the female anatomy, the uterus and fallopian tubes, never form. People with this syndrome often learn they have it only when they see a doctor to find out why they aren't menstruating.

Jenny's condition, called DHT deficiency, is a result of the body's inability to make one type of androgen, DHT, from testosterone itself. DHT guides the masculinization of the external genitals before birth, so the lack of DHT makes children born with this condition look like girls from the outside. But testosterone itself is still doing a job on cells all over the body. The hormone sets a hidden timer in the body, preparing it to display adult male traits at adolescence. When this time bomb of incipient manliness explodes in the teenage years, it can make for a particularly gruesome puberty. Confronted with maleness that they can strain to conceal but can't ignore, girls with DHT deficiency are forced to reexamine their sexual role in life.

How well girls are able to deal with this predicament often has more to do with how well the change is accepted by their friends, family, and by society at large. In one community in the Dominican Republic, DHT deficiency was relatively common, and the village easily accepted girls who became boys as teenagers. In another community in New Guinea, where the syndrome was also more common, they had strict separation of the sexes and imbued each gender with a fear of their opposite. Needless to say, children who switched genders have not been welcomed in the New Guinea village.

Clearly there is more than one element to sexuality. There is a genetic element (X and Y chromosomes), a biological element (genitals and secondary sexual characteristics), a sexual element (sexual preferences), and a social element (the social roles people play). Although women with androgen insensivity are male in a genetic sense, throughout their lives they remain completely female in every other way: socially, sexually, and biologically. Most people will never be able to tell if their genetic sex is out of sync with the rest of their lives. But what happens when a sexual purity test is applied and you are found genetically wanting?

Privates on Parade

Since 1968, the use of genetic testing has become widely accepted as a way of catching men who try to compete in women's sports events. It was introduced that year at the Tokyo Olympics and touted as a more modest and diplomatic alternative to having women parade naked in front of doctors. Some may chalk it up to the test's deterrent value that no men have been caught masquerading as women. But even before the genetic test, there was only one case of a man dressing as a woman to compete in the Olympics, a German high jumper who was caught after the 1936 games and claimed the Nazis forced him to perpetrate the sham (he placed fourth in his event).

Those who have been caught in the wide net of genetic testing include many women who have even a tiny piece of the Y chromosome in their gene pool. Every Olympics, the test exposes about 1 in 500 female athletes as genetic males or having male genes. At the 1984 Olympic games in Los Angeles, 6 out of about 2,500 women were disqualified based on genetic tests, according to an article in the British Journal of Sports Medicine. Most, if not all, of these women were learning about their condition for the first time.

If what scientists have learned about genetics and gender has generated some controversy, it is tiny compared to the confusion and emotionality created by a newly blooming field of research: the biology of sexual behavior.

Brain Sex

From very early in pregnancy, genes, proteins, and hormones conspire to sculpt the embryo into boy or girl. Chemicals in the fetus's blood install the right sexual plumbing. They flip the biological switches on billions of cells, wiring them so that, when adolescence hits, they will fire up all the secondary sexual machinery: changing breasts, hips, beards, voices.

But there is one sexual organ that is usually not considered when thinking about the biology of reproduction: the brain. After all, sex requires not only the right plumbing, but the desire, and the means, to hook the hoses together. Sexual reproduction requires that certain features of the opposite sex stimulate a flash of recognition deep in the brain and kindle the fires of attraction. Successful reproduction necessitates that an infant's round face and shrill cry evoke emotions of caring and concern.

We have already seen how hormones and other chemical signals shape and tailor boys' and girls' bodies for the different roles they will play when they reach adolescence and beyond. Do the chemical signals that separate boys and girls physically also operate on the brain in the womb? How much of our sexual selves is the result of changes in the brain that are laid down before birth? How many of our longings, our desires owe their existence to decisions developing nerve cells make before we are born—decisions made under the heady influence of the cocktail of sexual chemicals floating through the embryo?

Increasing evidence from animal and human studies in behavior, anatomy, and genetics indicates that what happens in the womb may have more effect on our sexual selves as adults than we realize.

Animal Passions

In 1959, Robert Goy and his colleagues at the University of Wisconsin–Madison, performed a surprising experiment. They gave pregnant rats male or female hormones, and then looked for effects of these sex hormones in the rat pups. The physical gender of the pups remained unchanged, but the scientists found that their sexual behavior was reversed. Male rats exposed to female hormones before birth started acting like females, and females exposed to male hormones started acting like males. It was the first hint that sexual behavior was not irrevocably tied to gender, at least in a laboratory setting.

Do those effects also work in nature? It's one thing to smack animals with an artificial blast of hormones more appropriate to the opposite sex, but can natural fluctuations in hormonal levels in the womb change development and affect adult behavior? In other words, can natural fluctuations decide whether males are studs or duds? It turns out that in gerbils and other rodents this is definitely the case.

Professors Mertice Clark and Bennet Galef, Jr. studied

the sexual success of Mongolian gerbils and correlated that information with their position in the womb during gestation. Gerbils are usually born in litters of six to seven, although as many as thirteen pups can be in one litter. At their laboratory at McMaster University in Hamilton, Ontario, Clark and Galef found that hormones emanating from the pups in the womb heavily affects the fertility and behavior of neighboring pups.

During the pregnancy, the gerbil pups are lined up along the two sides of the womb. Each gerbil pup may lie alongside pups of the same sex, the opposite sex, or one of each. Through analysis of thousands of litters, the two scientists found that when a female pup was wedged between two other females, the one in the center became a hot ticket. She became fertile much sooner and had larger litters than female pups flanked by males. She also adopted a reproductive strategy of quantity over quality: she was more willing to mate with strange males, and had litters more often, but she spent less time taking care of the young once she had them.

Conversely, males jammed between two other males in the womb made them supermasculine. The pups receiving the double hit of testosterone from their gerbil brothers grew up to be bigger, smellier, and heavier than other gerbils. They also were sexual swingers who fathered larger litters. On the other hand, males flanked by females in the womb turned out to be something of duds. "We offer them all sorts of luscious females, but they just can't manage to get them pregnant," says Galef. "If they do get the females pregnant, their litter sizes are smaller."

What does all this mean for the human animal? After all, we like to think that we are at least a little different from gerbils, a little more complex in our sexual development. I mean, we aren't just sexual automatons, right? We're the most changeable and self-directed of all animals. We use our advanced brain to rise to a sexual/cognitive level far above that of rigidly programmed gerbils.

Right?

Child's Play

It's difficult to scientifically pin these results on humans, because it's hard or impossible to conduct the same experiments in humans that we can in animals. Humans aren't born in litters, and ethical considerations bar scientists from artificially manipulating a baby's exposure to sex hormones in the womb. There are natural conditions, however, that mimic such manipulations. Like so many other anomalies of nature, these are the exceptions that scientists hope will prove the rule.

One such condition is congenital adrenal hyperplasia

(CAH). In CAH, an enzyme that usually processes androgens into another hormone is missing or defective, leading to a buildup of androgens in the bloodstream. Babies with CAH are usually diagnosed shortly after birth, and treatments are begun that can correct the hormonal imbalances for the rest of their lives. But these children have already been exposed to unusually high levels of male hormones in the womb.

Melissa Hines, a neuroscientist at the University of London, is interested in how hormones affect sex-typical behavior. She is one of many scientists who is interested in studying the behavior of CAH girls and boys to see if the changed prenatal hormone levels affect how they play by themselves and with others.

Hines and her colleagues devised an experiment in which scientists outfitted an observation room with various toys, including more stereotypically "boy toys" (construction equipment, toy guns), stereotypically "girl toys" (dolls, toy household equipment), and active-play equipment (a mini trampoline, "Bobo" the punching bag). Children with CAH and "control" children without the disorder were then set loose in the room in various combinations, and the scientists observed their play through a one-way mirror. The observers did not know which children had CAH and which did not.

Not surprisingly, the boys in the control group, those

without CAH, played more often with the "boy" toys and tended to choose to play with other boys. Girls in the control group most often played with the "girl" toys and chose to play with other girls. But, Hines also found, girls with CAH (those exposed to high concentrations of masculinizing androgens in the womb) were more likely than the girls without CAH to favor masculine toys and to play with boys. They were also more likely to be described as "tomboys." The boys with CAH didn't seem to be appreciably different from the boys in the control group, a result that would be predicted from similar animal studies, says Hines.

With the CAH children, Hines and other scientists have found that humans are no special case—as with other animals, human hormonal levels in the womb seem to affect later behavior. This work has been backed up by similar results with hormones that were prescribed for expecting mothers.

This is particularly important in light of recent information about hormones in the environment: it turns out that chemicals that mimic the female sex hormone estrogen are nearly everywhere in modern society. They are in pesticides, household chemicals, and other products we come in contact with every day. No behavioral effects of these estrogenic chemicals have been discovered yet, but epidemiological studies have led some scientists to blame the decrease in male fertility over the last few decades on increased exposure to estrogenic chemicals while males were in their mothers' womb.

How could hormones in the womb affect later behavior? The obvious answer would be that they change the brain somehow, that hormones influence the growing brain so that its wiring favors certain responses over others. Are men and women so different because their brains are made differently? Do they think differently because the basic machinery of their thoughts is different? Researchers have looked for these brain differences in humans, and they are beginning to find them.

Body of Knowledge

Until the late 1960s, scientists assumed that male and female brains were exactly alike. Sure, different species had different brain plans, and even in the same species there were subtle differences in the wrinkles that run along the surface of the brain—but in every species both males and females seemed to have exactly the same brain structures.

Then two scientists in Britain, Geoffrey Raisman and Pauline Field, began looking more closely at the hypothalamus, an area of the brain that controls sexual responses and appears to interact strongly with circulating hormones. Using an electron microscope, they counted nerve connections in part of the hypothalamus from both male and female rats. They counted over half a million connections, and when the data was tabulated they found a clear sex difference between males and females.

Their next experiment was to castrate male rats at birth and give the females testosterone. This had already been shown to reverse sexual behavior, making males act like female and vice versa. They then repeated their counting experiments on these rats. They found that the hormones had also reversed the connections in the hypothalamus, giving males a female pattern, and females a male pattern. So hormones can change the structure of the brain, presumably changing individual inclinations at the same time.

Since then, other scientists have found other sex differences in a wide variety of species—including humans. For most people, research on anatomical gender differences in humans first burst onto their personal radar screens in 1991, when a researcher at the Salk Institute in La Jolla, California, found not only a brain difference between men and women, but also between homosexual and heterosexual men.

Mounting Evidence

One of the behaviors that gets switched in gender-reversed rodents is sexual attraction: hormone-treated females will try and mount other females. Sex-reversed males will ex-

hibit "lordosis," a female position that tells males, in effect, "come on up and see me sometime." Given that there
is behavioral reversal in animals who also have changes in
brain anatomy, it seems reasonable to wonder if gay men
and lesbians also have measurable differences in their
brain structure.

In the late 1980s, Simon LeVay, the Salk Institute researcher, began comparing that all-important hypothalamus in women and gay and straight men. He discovered
that one part of the hypothalamus, called the third in-
terstitial nucleus (INAH3), was usually about twice as
large in men as it is in women. Except for in gay men.
Their INAH3 was more like a woman's. The rule was
not absolute: some heterosexual men had a small INAH3
and some gay men and straight women had a larger one.
But generally their INAH3 sizes clustered in the same
size range.

The work has to be reproduced by other scientists, and
LeVay himself cautions that all the gay men in the study
were infected with AIDS, which may have changed the results. Generally, however, the scientific community feels
that the work seems reliable and could easily be backed
up by future research. The finding, after all, fits in well
with research on animal behavior and anatomy, and
changes in the brain might be one way that "gay" genes
(of which other researchers have begun to find evidence)
might operate.

What is the picture that emerges from this human and animal research? As scientists learn more, somehow things get less clear. For most mammals, what goes on in the womb seems to have a strong effect on the structure of the brain and the animals' subsequent behavior. For people, there is a growing body of evidence that there are biological differences in the way men and women think and that there is also a "womb effect" that seems to influence sexual and non-sexual behaviors. But just how strong this effect is, and how permanent it is, remains in doubt. Even when the brain is sculpted by hormones in the womb, it is modified by experiences and hormones after birth. "One must be careful not to think that such differences are fixed and can never be changed," says British scientist Geoffrey Raisman in the *Journal of NIH Research*. "The brain is not a lump of marble cut out by God. It is a living structure continually changing itself."

The implications of new knowledge about the hormonal effects on babies in the womb are also hard to assess. For one thing, it's not easy to see where womb effects end, and other effects begin. But one basic problem seems to be that people can't decide whether humans should "go with the flow" of biological forces or oppose them. If a biological inclination toward homosexuality is found, does this legitimatize homosexuality? Or is it just another biological condition—like a tendency toward alcoholism—that deserves to be resisted? If boys are more inclined to wreck things, should that desire be indulged and limited—or should this information spur us to try even harder to change boys' behavior? If women are biologically inclined to be more emotionally changeable, should that bar them from roles that demand a high degree of emotional stability? Is overcoming biological restrictions what sets us apart from other animals, or does it breed alienation as we journey farther from our true natures?

Science and society haven't been able to answer these questions yet, and it seems likely that the babies currently lounging in their warm baths in the womb will still be struggling with the same dilemmas when their hair is turning gray.

Scientists will continue to supply fascinating information about the effects of life in the womb, and this information will settle some arguments and start many more. But it's unlikely that science will ever be able to take away the confusion and discord that have clouded issues of sex and sexuality for millennia.

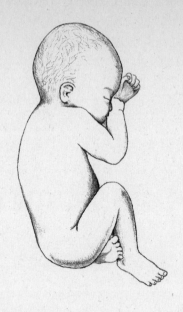

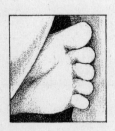

actual size

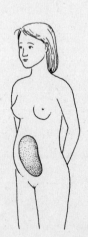

THE SEVENTH
MONTH

(Weeks 27–30 after conception;
weeks 29–31 after LMP)

During this month, the fetus matures enough that he stands a very good chance of surviving if born prematurely. By the end of this period, his lungs are capable of expanding and they have good surface area for letting oxygen pass into the blood. His central nervous system continues to mature, and the expanding brain begins to wrinkle to fit even more gray matter into the skull. The baby can now regulate body temperature. By week 28, all babies are startled by loud noises. Unlike the previous month, when there was a noticeable gap between the sound and the startled response, the baby now reacts to the noise in a fraction of a second.

During this time, bursts of nerve activity in the brain inundate the baby's brain in what seems to be REM (rapid eye movement) sleep, equivalent to our dream sleep. While in this REM sleep state, the eyes, ears, and other organs are stimulated, and the baby's heart rate and blood pressure change. At this point the baby spends 70 to 80 percent of his time in the REM state.

The baby also starts laying down fat during this period, smoothing out and filling out his wrinkly skin. By the end of the month, white fat is about 4 percent of his body weight. The baby's total weight at this point averages about 2 kilos (4.4 pounds).

The baby is getting very large for his living space now, and he can no longer move around much or flip in the womb. Many babies start to assume an upside-down position with the head pushing into the pelvic bowl. By the end of the month, he has grown to an average of 40 centimeters (15 inches) and is tucked up in a ball 30 centimeters long (12 inches). The fine hair (lanugo) that has covered his body now begins to disappear.

SEVEN

AWAKENINGS

Still slippery and purplish, the newborn squints at the bright, dry world and registers blurry lightforms. He hears the sounds in the room and can pick out his mother's voice. His arms and legs, suddenly free of the shrink-wrapped amniotic sac, flail and punch. He feels the coldness of the air after his long prenatal bath, then is reassured by the sweaty warmth of his mother's chest. His lips feel and draw toward the tip of the proffered breast, toward the sweet, liquid tapioca of the colostrum expressed at the nipple.

It seems intuitively likely that the ability to see, hear, and feel doesn't simply switch on at birth. Scientists have known for decades that all the senses the baby uses at birth have been in operation long before in the womb. Except for the sudden explosion of new sensations, there is no difference between what the baby can sense in the moments before birth and what she can sense in the first minutes after birth. There is no master switch thrown to turn on the senses when the baby is born.

So if babies can sense their surroundings in the womb, how do they perceive their world? And how and when do they acquire these senses, these abilities?

Through ultrasound and other imaging techniques, animal studies, sound reactivity tests and microphones placed in the womb, scientists in the last decade have been exploring this world, returning to the motherland to map its sights and sounds. They have found that uterine existence is a rich one, full of sounds, feelings, vibrations—even, occasionally, a tiny bit of light. They have also recorded how the baby learns from these stimuli, and how the sensory massage actually shapes the fetus and prepares it, physically and emotionally, for the outside world.

Life in Inner Space

If a baby can hear, feel, and see before birth, what does life seem like in the cozy confines of his waterbed? Vision, which is often the primary sense for humans in the post-natal world, is not so important before birth. Indeed, only a very little light filters into the womb at all. The light that seeps through the stretched skin of the abdomen is the same kind of light you see if you put a flashlight against the thin skin between your thumb and forefinger in a dark room. The light that passes through is dim and red, of little use for distinguishing features. But it *is* noticeable. Fetuses that are five months old will turn their head away from a bright light that is shone through the abdomen and into the womb.

Touch is a much more dominant sensation. In the womb, the rocking, washing massage of motion stimulates the baby. He feels the vibration of a jarring step and a growling stomach. In the third trimester he will sometimes respond to a gentle prod with an impish poke back. Sometimes the *lack* of motion will stimulate him to kick and punch, and movement will calm him.

Fetuses even seem to have a sense of taste. Scientists have shown that sugar solutions injected into the amniotic fluid make the baby increase the amount of fluid he swallows.

The preeminent sense at work in the womb, though, is hearing. The womb is awash with sound, and the baby is scanning and picking up the aural traffic like a ham radio operator. In the background are the constant thumps and gurgles that the mother's body makes as it carries out life's maintenance and housekeeping activities. There is the mechanical drum of the pumping heart, beating out a tune that is sometimes a frenzied fortissimo, sometimes a calming adagio. The squeezing and flexing of the working intestine produces the onomatopoetically named borborygmi: the groans and burbles of food being processed. The baby even hears the rhythmic whoosh-whoosh of blood sluicing through nearby arteries and the airy aspiration of the lungs filling and emptying.

His Master's Voice

Over these ambient noises drift sounds that will resonate and grow in importance over time: human voices, carrying messages from the outer space beyond the womb. In the final months before birth, these voices will reinforce the connection between the growing fetus and his fellow human beings, molding an emotional link that will be vital after birth. The strongest and clearest of these voices will be that of the mother, carried directly to the child through the fluid conduit of mom's body.

Scientists who place microphones inside the womb immediately before birth, after the amniotic membrane has ruptured, find that the transmission of sound is far from perfect. The skin and fat and fluid between the speaker and the sprite, plus the background body sounds in the womb, cut off about 30 decibels of sound from outside. The strength of a nearby human voice is about 65 to 70 decibels, so the intensity of voices from outside is almost cut in half. Add to that the fact that fluids absorb high frequency sounds most avidly, and the voices that do seep through to the baby are decidedly shifted to the bass clef.

The result is that the audio link carrying the sound of voices into the womb is about as good as a string stretched between two cans. What comes through best, scientists feel, is not the actual words spoken, but their cadence, their intonation, their volume and stress. William Fifer, a scientist at Columbia University who studies sounds in the womb, likens the voices heard in the womb to the sounds that come through a wall. "Speaking from my experience with New York apartments, if you hear a stereo from the apartment next door, you hear the rhythm of the drums and the bass, but not a lot of the other music."

The dominance of the mother's voice in the womb is suggested by experiments done by Fifer and his colleague Anthony J. DeCasper at the University of North Carolina at Greensboro. They rigged up an artificial nipple so that babies could control, by the rhythm of their sucking, whether a tape machine played the sound of their mother's voice or someone else's. One-day-old babies voted for mom's voice over any other. There was only one sound they preferred more: the sound of the mother's voice after it had been electronically modified to simulate the sound they used to hear in the womb.

The scientists also found that babies prefer the sound of other female voices over male voices, including that of the father. Fathers shouldn't despair, though, says Fifer. Male voices get the nod when the vote is between them and silence.

Scientists have other evidence to support the idea that the fetus is becoming acquainted with the rhythm and pitch of sounds from the outer world. DeCasper has found that newborns become very interested and attentive when they hear music that was repeatedly played for them before birth. DeCasper and others have found similar recognition reactions when newborns listened to the stories their mothers regularly read aloud while pregnant, or songs moms sang. Babies also prefer the sound of voices in the same language heard in the womb, probably because different languages have different rhythms and cadences.

Fifer is trying to use the information he is collecting to improve on a prenatal test called VAST (vibro-acoustic stimulation test). VAST assesses the baby's responses when a 95-decibel buzzer is set off on the mother's belly. "It's like going up and banging a cymbal next to their head," says Fifer. "The fetus jumps and his bladder empties." VAST is a fairly primitive test: It really measures whether basic startle responses are wired up in the nervous system. The fetus either jumps or he doesn't. Fifer would like to devise a more sensitive test of developmental progress using voices or other sounds and measuring the fetal heart rate.

But other than rhythm and stress how much language information does the fetus hear or register? Can he or she hear and distinguish between actual words in the womb? Scientists find it much harder to uncover evidence that the fetus can discern such differences. Moreover, there are good reasons to think the fetus misses most of this non-prosodic part of speech.

For one thing, all that background noise competes for the fetus' attention. Imagine trying to hear a conversation in the next room while you're standing next to a blender and a blaring stereo. You might be able to tell whether the conversation is angry or friendly, but you probably wouldn't be able to make out the actual words. For the fetus, the kinds of sounds that carry information about individual words and syllables are in exactly the frequency range inhabited by the loudest background noises, Fifer says, so that information may well be lost. Infants usually don't start paying particular attention to the sylla-bles common to their own language until a long time after birth.

On the other hand, two-day-old babies can notice when consonants switch order in a word, and five-day-olds can tell the difference between short syllables that differ only slightly. Some language sounds heard in the womb may contribute to these early abilities.

The sound preferences that babies only a few hours old show demonstrate that they have been learning a few things when whiling away their days in the womb. New-borns display all the characteristics of early learning: they recognize and respond differently to stimuli they have en-countered before. They also show another aspect of learn-ing called habituation: babies who jump at a loud sound will react less if the sound is repeated so that they get used to it.

But how much can a baby learn before birth?

Some people have used information about learning in the womb to sell what they call "prenatal universities." Expectant parents pay for courses that purport to teach their babies vocabulary in the womb. Scientists roundly scoff at these claims. Experiments done so far don't indi-cate that intensive exposure to stimuli will result in su-perbabies. "There is no evidence that any of this does any good," says Fifer. Harm may even result, he suggests, if the fetus is regularly exposed to the very loud volumes that are needed to bring words clearly into the womb. "I think it's pretty irresponsible for these people to prey on parents' desire to provide the best for their baby."

Even though it's unlikely that babies can learn language in the womb, it doesn't take away from the wonder of everything they can sense and learn. How and when does the fetus come by this amazing consciousness? Scientists have been studying this intensively only in the last decade. They have found some astounding answers.

A Sentimental Education

By the time he is ready for birth, a baby has been restricted to his dark incubator for more than nine months. And although he has never left his watery swaddling, he has already taken a journey of unimaginable distance.

Starting first as one cell, then a cluster of cells, the pre-embryo had little sense of its surroundings, it merely drifted in the uterine fluid, tugged along by currents, with no compass and no guide. The fragile sprite of plasm followed the simple dictates of survival—it didn't yet have the need or the means to learn, to organize, or to make sense of the stimuli that washed over it. It didn't note or assign meaning to the beat of the mother's heart, or the pulse of her blood, or the sway of her walk. Yet from the mechanistic behavior of those first cells came an awareness, a sentience.

Those who ponder this incredible transformation are finding that, for the fetus, the process of coming to his senses, of awakening to the world around him, is also a process of learning. It is learning that takes place on the most basic, biological level, a bodily learning that molds the neural circuits of the fetus, makes the senses possible, and prepares the child for interacting emotionally and physically with his family.

In previous chapters, we've seen how the body and brain shape themselves as the embryo, and then the fetus, develops. The basic tools of the senses are crafted according to internal plans, without reference to the world outside the body. The crinkled flower of the ear blooms whether there is anything to hear or not. The nose knows nothing of perfume in the womb, but that little olfactory knob puckers up on the newly formed face nonetheless.

The challenge is that once these sensory organs are formed, they must be connected to the brain in a useful way. In order to categorize and learn from sensations, the brain has to be able to make sense of the signals it receives. This must happen before a newborn can recognize his mother's voice or taste her milk.

The brain and body do this through repetition and

practice. For example, research shows that once the ear and all the acoustic nerve cells are made, they send a jumble of signals to the brain through a tangle of nerve pathways. But the brain has a singular ability. It sorts signals by what they have in common. When one note hits the ear, it triggers hundreds of nerve signals to the brain. At first the brain cannot distinguish these signals from the random static of other nerve signals from the ear. But the brain circuitry takes note that certain signals arrive at the same time, and strengthens the connections that receive those signals. It learns to pick out the collection of nerve signals that represent the single note.

This process is similar to the way we can look at a car and notice a particular collection of features—a certain curve of the hood, the shape of the grille—and discern the pattern that tells us what kind of car it is. The incoming information creates a neural category that grows more defined each time that type of car is seen. As the neural connection grows stronger, the brain learns to ignore the random background.

By this method, the developing brain learns to associate particular patterns of nerve signals not only with one note, but with all notes, sounds, and sensations.

Through this process, the fetus blossoms into a sensuous being in response to the sensations of the world around it. The body plan provides the hardware for hearing, but the meaning of sounds is taught by the sounds themselves. The ears would form even if the womb were silent—although they might not work at birth.

The beauty of the system is that it works well for recognizing and learning all sorts of patterns. Besides sounds, the jostle and nudge of the mother's movement may teach the baby something about the mechanics of movement. Scientists have observed that babies born to mothers who are confined to bed for much of the pregnancy are often temporarily a little behind in the development of their own movements.

The system of making new neural connections may be important for an unfolding emotional awareness, too. Some scientists speculate that the sounds of the mother's voice, when associated with a sensation of being well fed and cared for in the womb, may help the child form an emotional bond with the mother after birth. The child may hear the stress of a fearful or angry moment in utero and associate it with the effects of stress hormones that cross the placenta and enter the fetal bloodstream. These sorts of associations may help a newborn later interpret his mother's level of stress by the cadence and frequency of her voice. In support of this is the finding that low-frequency sounds calm newborns, while high-frequency sounds induce stress. If the general hypothesis is true, it would mean that a mother's expressions of love, anger,

fear, and happiness might all be a positive part of the prenatal experience, all necessary to let the newborn know
his mother's emotional frame of mind and respond appropriately. This would give babies a head start on knowing
how to manipulate their parents into giving them what
they want and need.

But are senses formed only through the interaction
between sensation and sensory organ, between ear and
sound, between eye and light? After all, there is almost
nothing that can be seen in the near total darkness of the
womb, and yet the eyes do open, look, and see immediately after birth. How can the eyes perform immediately
if they haven't practiced beforehand? How does this fit
with the idea that the sensations of prenatal experience
teach the baby how to sense? Could there really be sense
organs that switch on at birth?

The surprising solution to this puzzle seems to lie in
recent research that indicates that the eyes teach themselves the basics of seeing. Lacking light to see, they supply their own light simulator. The implications of this may
be far-reaching, eventually helping us understand the nature of dreaming and perhaps even giving us a window
into the experience of life in the womb.

To explain the eye's self-education, it may be best
to turn briefly to an analogy: the process that occurs every
time you switch on a desktop computer.

Booting Up

In the Smithsonian Institution's National Museum of American History in Washington, D.C., there is a computer console the size of a car flipped on its side. Its face is studded with rows of dials, each surrounded by a spray of numerals from one to ten. In the late 1940s, such consoles used to fill whole rooms, even though this miracle of the atomic age, the ENIAC, was less powerful than today's simplest desktop computer. To make a calculation, the technicians first had to turn each dial to the proper numeral; the settings were read off a printed sheet. These settings were the primary software for the machine, what we now call the operating system.

A revolutionary advancement many years later was the invention of a computer that sent operating instructions to itself. Merely turning on the computer put current through the hardware and caused the computer to install its own operating system. Computer scientists said the computer was "pulling itself up by its own bootstraps," which became "booting up."

Carla Shatz, who studies the developing visual system at the University of California, Berkeley, has discovered that the fetal retina sends out signals that enable the visual system and its connections to the brain to "boot up." Shatz studies cats, but she says the basic pattern of eye development she sees is probably found in humans and other mammals.

After birth, when light hits the retina, photosensitive pigments convert the light signals into nerve signals. These signals pass through various nerve tracts and processing stations on the way back to the visual cortex, the outer rind of the brain that lies inside the rearmost part of the skull. Part of the visual cortex is almost like a movie screen. An image on the retina stimulates nerve signals to project a similar image of nerve activity in the visual cortex. If two spots lying next to each other on the retina are activated by light, two spots lying next to each other at the back of the brain will be activated. Mental pictures are formed.

The problem is that early in fetal brain development, there are no "dedicated connections" between those spots in the retina and those at the back of the brain. Experience is the stimulus that teaches the brain which connections to make. But, as we already know, there is almost no light in the womb to provide that experience.

The solution is that the retina creates its own signals without light. Shatz has documented waves of nerve activity that wash over the developing retina. These waves of activity then throw nerve signals back through the visual circuits of the brain, providing the critical experience necessary to train the brain. The eyes and the brain learn to see in the absence of light—by supplying the signals that light would, if it could. Like the computer, the eyes send the signals that supply the operating rules the brain needs to see. When the eyes at last open after birth, they are already prepared for use.

This process of "booting up" the brain is so elegant that researchers believe it must be used for other sensory systems, too. After all, there are so many brain systems that should be on-line and ready to work immediately after birth, if the newborn is to have the best possible chances of survival. In fact, there are suggestions that "booting up" is used not just for the senses, but throughout the brain, in its intellectual and emotional circuits as well. The process may, in fact, work on one of the most significant milestones of development in the womb, one noticed directly by Mom.

Bumping Bolero

Sometime in the fifth month, and sometimes even in the fourth, expecting mothers get a strange sensation. It may feel like an insect landing on the belly, or butterflies *in* the belly. Some describe it as feeling like the swish of a fish-tail. The feeling may be confusing for a fraction of a second, but most mothers have been waiting to feel this first nudge for some time and they are thrilled when it happens. Like Ravel's *Bolero,* the movements that can barely be perceived at first will slowly and steadily grow over the weeks and months until they demand constant notice.

This first sensation of movement is called "the quickening," because "quick" used to be a common synonym for living or alive. "Cut to the quick" therefore means "cut to within an inch of your life." The "quick and the dead" doesn't refer to pedestrians in New York City, but to two opposing groups—those who are still with us and those who have shuffled off their mortal coil. In pregnancy, the quickening was thought to mark the time when the fetus came alive.

Now we know that movements start much earlier than the fourth or fifth month, they just aren't strong enough to be felt until then. The development of ultrasound imaging has given scientists surprising insights into just how early the baby does start moving. By the sixth week after conception (eighth week after LMP), the embryo can be observed arching his back and neck, lifting himself off the bottom of the amniotic sac for a moment, before slowly settling back down.

One week later, ultrasound can be used to spot motion in the just-sprouting arms and legs. The embryo probably makes other movements too subtle for ultrasound earlier. In fact, the first measurable motion might be considered the contractions of the heart, which begin as soon as the heart-tube is constructed on the 23rd day of gestation (in the sixth week after LMP).

The general principle of muscle development seems to be that as soon as there is something to move, as soon as there is a nerve attached to a muscle, it moves. But how? For a long time, scientists assumed that movements were reflexes—automatic responses to touches from the amniotic sac. But in recent years it has become clear that these are not reflexes. Like the brain systems that stimulate themselves to "boot up," the first muscle movements are the result of self-generated nerve impulses, not reflexive reactions to stimulation. (Later in gestation, when motor function is more developed, the movements can be reactions to stimulation.)

The other surprise is that these self-generated signals are not coming from the brain. When scientists looked for the origin of the movement, they found the signals originated in the spinal cord. Early in gestation, the spinal cord seems to act as a primitive brain which coordinates movement. The neurons start by firing randomly, and when they start moving in the seventh week the limbs move together. But then the neurons in the spinal cord begin to separate nerve signals belonging to separate limbs. By the eighth or ninth week (tenth or eleventh week after

LMP), the arms and legs are able to move independently of each other.

As time passes, the fetus' movements become smoother and more organized and show more signs of reactivity. By the twelfth week, the fetus moves in response to something brushing his skin. By the halfway point in the pregnancy, the limbs have begun to move in more complex patterns and the hips, knees, elbows, and ribs are flexing. This movement actually sculpts the structure of the growing joints so that they fit together smoothly.

One of these pattern of movement is called "stepping," a circular motion of the legs that resembles walking or riding an invisible bicycle. As the pregnancy comes to a close and the baby starts filling out his living quarters, the stepping action seems to help him to flip around until his head gets caught in the upside-down position, where he will start preparing for his exit into the outside world.

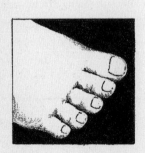

actual size

THE EIGHTH MONTH

*(Weeks 31–34 after conception;
weeks 33–36 after LMP)*

By this time, the pace of development is slow as the fetus starts to complete work on all the major body systems. Babies born prematurely at this stage have an extremely good chance of survival. The baby's central nervous system had matured enough so that it is directing breathing motions and performing reflexes such as narrowing the pupils in response to light. He is also able to change the eyes' focus and blink. By the end of the month, the baby's muscles are constantly contracting and relaxing. He is spending more than 80 percent of his time "breathing" amniotic fluid.

The baby looks pinkish and smooth now that a good layer of fat has been laid down under the skin. In the last two and a half months, the baby fully doubles his weight, and much of the new bulk is fat. By the end of this month, the fetus weighs around 2.5 kilos (5.5 pounds), and 7 to 8 percent of his body weight is fat. At this point, the baby is usually about 45 centimeters long (18 inches), and measures about 32 centimeters (13 inches) from head to rump.

EIGHT

UNDRESSED REHEARSAL

IN GREEK MYTHOLOGY, ATHENA, PATRON GODDESS OF ATHENS, sprang fully formed from the forehead of Zeus. As the last months drag and the expectant mother longs to sleep on her stomach once again and burn her maternity clothes, she may wish her baby could come into the world the way Athena did: bursting forth instantly from her forehead—or perhaps even better—from his *father's* forehead.

Always short of breath, and at pains to get anywhere, the mother will wonder how it's possible for her little dumpling to get much bigger. He is already shoving aside her vital organs left and right, north and south, elbowing the liver, shouldering the intestines, and kicking the bladder. If pregnancy were basketball, he would have already fouled out of the game. As it is, the game is more like basketbelly—and Shorty gets to take regular penalty shots at mom.

Other than a steady and surprising increase in size, little seems to be happening during these last months. And though the baby's developmental changes are not as dramatic as they were in the first few months, this time is nonetheless crucial.

The last chapter discussed how the baby spends this period training his senses and begins to hear, smell, feel, and even see. We saw that development is a continuum, that there is no sudden change in cognition or awareness at birth. But birth does present an enormous physical challenge. From the time the baby emerges from the warm, dark, birth canal, he has to survive on his own in the harsh light of day. In the cooler, dry air he must immediately warm his own body after months of bathing in the easy spa of mommy's tummy. He must also rustle up his own food once the gravy train of the umbilical cord has been cut, forcing him to exercise muscles and senses that have never been used before. Oh, the shock of it all! He won't likely experience such trauma again until the day he leaves home. How does the baby acquire the ability to hold the world at bay, to ward off its dangers and to make it fill his needs?

All of the jolts and strains of birth demand endurance training in the womb. They require bodybuilding—babybuilding—that will allow the newborn not just to survive, but to thrive in a difficult world. As with the senses, the baby prepares for the future by working out—by exercising, while still in the womb, the very skills he will need after birth. Before the first zephyr of air brushes his face, his chest begins to heave in a slow breathing motion. Before a drop of milk washes into his mouth, he is swallowing and conditioning his stomach and intestines for future meals. He is bracing himself against the cold and the presence of germs. He is putting every part and system in his body through a dress rehearsal for opening night, for independence day.

Inspiration

The baby in the womb is a mammal submerged; like a deep-sea diver, his air link to the atmospheric world comes through a hose. Unlike a diver's air hose, though, the umbilical cord carries fluid, already enriched with oxygen after its side trip through the placenta. The lungs built to oxygenate the blood, on the other hand, remain un-used and are filled with amniotic fluid. But they are not in-active. Months before delivery, the baby begins preparing for the critical moment when someone will cut the cord and he is momentarily without an oxygen supply. Every-thing rests on his ability to make a startled gulp and draw in the very first of 800 million breaths. To get ready for this moment, the lungs have been in training. At about the 24th week of pregnancy, the baby starts mimicking the action of breathing, inhaling and exhaling amniotic fluid from the sac that surrounds him. The movement exercises the breathing muscles and helps them become coordinated.

This breathing in the womb doesn't happen all the time, however. Strangely enough, it occurs only during the phase of sleep known as rapid eye movement (REM) sleep (see Chapter 5), when the brain stem dispatches nerve signals across the brain and the eyes flick back and forth. During the last trimester, the baby is in REM sleep over half of the time.

After birth, it is during REM sleep that dreams visit us. The more romantic among us might suggest that the fetus breathes because he is dreaming of the future, of a world filled with air instead of fluid. But it's more likely that the centers of the brain that are stimulating REM are also stim-ulating the part of the brain that controls breathing, prepar-ing it for the time it will need to go on autopilot.

The discovery in the early 1970s that the fetus actually inhales and exhales gave scientists a new view of the fetus, says Dr. Henrique Rigatto, who studies fetal breathing at the University of Manitoba, Winnipeg. "Before this, scientists generally saw fetal development as a passive process," Rigatto says. Scientists began to look more closely at the ways in which the baby acts and reacts in the womb, especially late in pregnancy. They began to observe the fetus's concerted actions and behaviors in the same way they studied the behaviors of newborns and children.

Life's a Feast

The unborn baby's lively existence includes another unexpected activity: eating. Of course, the fetal diet is necessarily liquid—there are no pizzas delivered in utero—but he is really quite a guzzler. In the last trimester, the fetus slurps up as much as 750 milliliters of the surrounding amniotic fluid every day, about one-third of his body weight near term. That's the equivalent of a 120-pound adult drinking nearly five gallons of Gatorade a day. Some of the swallowed fluid passes into the mother's body via the umbilical cord. Another portion is simply peed back out into the amniotic sac.

Sean Mulvihill, a physician and researcher at the University of California, San Francisco, has been using animal models to study how this heavy drinking affects the fetus. He has found that slurping up amniotic fluid is an important part of development, a vital part of the training regimen that readies the baby for life in the outside world. Mulvihill and his colleagues have found that the amniotic fluid passing through the fetus' stomach and intestines actually helps those tissues grow properly. Mulvihill noticed that, in rabbits, if the fetus doesn't swallow amniotic fluid, intestinal growth and maturation slows. After birth, these rabbits have lower-than-normal levels of digestive acids and enzymes. "Amniotic fluid contains a potent, but as yet unidentified, growth factor," says Mulvihill. Discovery and isolation of this growth factor could help doctors heal ulcers and other wounds in the adult gastro-intestinal tract.

Mulvihill and his colleagues also found that the baby's swallowing isn't all practice. The amniotic fluid contains substantial, high-calorie nutrients, including sugars and protein. In spite of the fact that the placenta and the umbilical cord seem able to supply the baby with all the food he needs, Mulvihill calculates that amniotic fluid supplies about 10 percent to 14 percent of the nutritional requirement of the normal fetus.

The finding that the placenta doesn't have to bring home all the bacon is significant. If there are problems with the placenta, they can reduce the baby's nutrient supply, limiting his growth. This can cause a condition called intrauterine growth retardation (IUGR), in which an otherwise normal infant is born, at term, weighing 2,500 grams (5.5 pounds) or less. Infants born with severe growth retardation are at a greater risk of infections and neurological handicaps. But if the amniotic fluid the baby swallows offers a backup source of nutrition, it may minimize the consequences of a defective placenta by introducing supplemental nutrients directly into the womb.

Body Armor

Once the baby consumes the groceries, he needs to start laying something away, in the form of fat, for the future. After birth, babies will not eat much for the first few days, and they have to live off the fats they have stored away in utero. In addition, the fat offers protection against the cold. White fat, the kind we are most familiar with, is an insulating layer like the blubber that keeps whales and walruses cozy in the arctic. Brown fat, as discussed in Chapter 3, also keeps babies warm. This type of fat is packed with the energy transducers called mitochondria, which allow calories stored in the fat to be turned into heat right on the spot. White fat is mostly siphoned off to other cells in order to turn its energy into heat. Brown fat commonly warms hibernating animals. The fetus starts putting on brown fat in certain places early, at about the 18th week of pregnancy.

The baby starts salting away white fat stores about two months later. As mentioned earlier, until he does, his skin is wrinkled and thin, giving him the appearance of a wizened old man. Up to this point, the baby literally seems like skin and bones with the wall of his skin stretched so thinly over his body that blood vessels and the ghostly images of bones can be easily seen.

At about the twenty-sixth week (during the seventh month), the baby starts putting on white fat and bulking up in earnest. By the thirtieth week, the average fetus has padded himself with almost 2 ounces of fat, which represents about 3.5 percent of his total body weight. Four weeks later, he has put on almost four times as much fat. After a full term in the womb when the baby is ready to be born, he has gathered a chunky 15 percent of his weight in body fat. The fat stores are then available as a rich source of energy and warmth. Typically, babies lose some weight in the first few days after birth; most of that weight is lost fat and water.

In the last few months before birth, the fetus is also girding itself with another extremely important defense: the immunological armor that will shield him from disease. Even before birth, while the baby is surrounded by the sterile bath of amniotic fluid, he will be threatened by disease-causing organisms that slip past the mother's defenses and sneak across the placenta. Immediately after birth, foreign organisms will swarm across his body, even in the cleanest hospital room. Most of these organisms aren't what we usually think of as harmful. But even the bacteria that benignly settle on our skin and in our lungs every day can cause illness when the immune system isn't functioning, and a baby's immune system isn't brought up to full steam until months after birth.

To guard against these wayward invaders, the fetus borrows some of his mother's personal immunological experience. Like the rotating bookshelves that open onto a hidden passage in old mystery movies, special proteins embedded in the placenta grab antibodies from mom's bloodstream and pull them across the placental barrier and into the baby's blood supply. These immune molecules represent the biological memories of all the pathogens the mother has had the misfortune to bump into in her lifetime. If any alien molecules, bacteria, protozoa, or viruses that have threatened her before manage to make it across the placenta, the newly relocated antibodies in the baby's bloodstream stand prepared to latch on to them. Once they have a grip on the enemy, the antibodies can surround them, bind many of them together into a big ineffectual logjam, or call in other molecules to help destroy them.

Scientists are beginning to discover that, at least in

some cases, physicians can provide the fetus with a sort of short-term vaccination. In a study conducted in the early 1990s by scientists around the United States, pregnant women were given vaccinations against haemophilus influenza type B, a sometimes lethal bacterial infection that can cause pneumonia and meningitis in newborns. This microbe is the leading bacterial killer of children in the United States. The scientists found evidence that after receiving the shot, mothers created antibodies to protect themselves against the deadly bug and passed that antibody protection along to their unborn babies. They also found that the prenatal vaccination could provide protection against the microbe for six months, enough time for the baby's own immune system to start functioning. These scientists believe that after further development and testing, such prenatal vaccinations could be used against a number of diseases.

What happens to a baby born without enough of the armor designed to protect him? What happens when the baby's rehearsal is cut short, when he is shoved out on stage too soon? Medical science has learned a lot about what it takes to create a halfway house for the fetus until he is ready to fend for himself.

High-Tech Womb

Electronic monitors, oxygen bottles, drip meters, plasma and blood, a ventilator, a dialysis machine, and a cart full of syringes, tubing, forceps, bandages, scissors, and other medical paraphernalia surround the single table in the neonatal intensive care unit at the Lucile Salter Packard Children's Hospital at Stanford University. From all directions flow multicolored wires and clear tubes, connecting the machines to the small tabletop with a nest of cotton towels at its center. From four feet above, a white spotlight beams down on a living jewel, a pink, miniature girl curled at the center of a $200,000 chrome and plastic cradle. Born two months too early, she weighs just over two pounds. Her entire body is only two hand-lengths. Her head, the size of an apple, is swathed in a knit cap and gauze covers her eyes. A gauze-covered board is strapped to her left forearm where an intravenous line enters. As she warms in the spotlight, she makes involuntary movements, leg kicks and arm waves.

Across the room, surrounded by an identical array of machines, another tiny baby lies in darkness, asleep. The boy has short, dark hair covering his whole body, and he is so small that he could curl up on top of a book. This little one warms in a plastic box covered by a towel. The lights on the monitors and a stretch of blood-filled tubing—no bigger than vermicelli—snaking over the top of the incubator are the only exterior reminders of the soul in the machine and the mortal struggle going on inside.

This is the third trimester of pregnancy, exposed. In these beds and the dozen or so others around the ward lie not infants so much as fetuses outside the womb. When babies leave the womb prematurely, technology becomes the midwife for their survival, and doctors and nurses scramble to keep up with the babies' needs. In the process of caring for premature babies, physicians are getting a look at life during the last trimester. As doctors labor to minimize bleeding in fragile tissue, regulate breathing in walnut-sized lungs, and monitor a thousand other vital factors, they are getting a fast-paced course in how to be a distant second-best to a mother's womb. They have learned a great deal in the two decades since a tragedy focused national attention on premature birth and helped form the field of neonatology.

A Lung Too Young

On August 7, 1963, a pregnant Jacqueline Kennedy felt a stabbing pain while watching her children take riding lessons in Hyannis, Massachusetts. With one miscarriage and one stillbirth behind her, and with more than a month before her due date, she must have felt dread for the child inside her. The First Lady was taken by helicopter to a hospital at the nearby Otis Air Force Base, and the President rushed from Washington to join her. At the hospital, a four-pound, ten-ounce boy was born by cesarean section, five and a half weeks premature. Because his young lungs were too stiff and shriveled to draw enough oxygen into his tiny body, the boy immediately started having trouble breathing. He fell prey to a condition then called hyaline membrane syndrome—now commonly called respiratory distress syndrome (RDS). His physicians dashed him to the Children's Medical Center in Boston, where they felt they could give him better care. The President's son was placed in a pressurized oxygen chamber and given antibiotics to stave off pneumonia. As his condition worsened, a priest arrived and baptized him Patrick Bouvier Kennedy. On August 9th, after thirty-six hours in which he struggled for each breath, the young Kennedy succumbed to the syndrome.

His death came at the beginning of the modern era of preemie care. One sad aspect of this tragedy was that infant ventilators—the machines that push air in and out of the lungs—were just coming into use on an experimental basis in a few university medical centers. Such ventilators weren't yet being used at the hospital where the President's son was taken. "If Patrick had been born at Vanderbilt University, McGill University, University of Colorado, or Stanford University, he might have survived," notes

David Stevenson, the head of the neonatal intensive care unit at the Lucile Salter Packard Children's Hospital.

Doctors at Stanford University and elsewhere had discovered that they just couldn't use adult ventilators on infants. Infants breathe faster (at about forty to sixty breaths a minute, versus 12–20 breaths per minute in adults) and have different air volume and air flow needs. Ventilators for infants have now become very advanced. They can virtually vibrate the air in and out of newborns, pulsing very small bursts of air through their lungs hundreds of times per minute.

But in the 1960s and 1970s, when ventilators were still primitive, physicians discovered they had another problem: the ventilators themselves were causing damage by forcing open collapsed lungs. It can be tremendously difficult to inflate a collapsed lung in a premature infant because the sides of the lung stick together under the influence of surface tension—the same force that makes two plates of glass stick tightly together when there is a little water between them. In full-term infants, children, and adults, lung collapse is prevented by a detergent-like molecule called surfactant. But the lungs don't start making surfactant until about the twenty-eighth week of pregnancy and don't finish until the last week of term. Without surfactant, the microscopic lung sacs called alveoli collapse every time the baby exhales, and like uninflated balloons, the sacs resist expanding again. In order to get more air into the lungs, ventilators must force air into young lungs that are not yet ready for pressure. Doctors have tried to make up for preemies' breathing problems by having them breathe oxygen-rich air, but too much oxygen itself can also damage the lungs.

The alveoli, deprived of surfactant, also act like balloons in another unfortunate way. Balloons are hard to blow up at first, but once you get some air in them it becomes a lot easier to fill them. The implication of this for the premature lung can be seen with a simple experiment. If you blow into a Y-shaped tube that connects to two balloons, one balloon will always start expanding first. As it expands, it takes in more air more easily, making it less likely that the other balloon will ever get started. Eventually, if you keep blowing, one balloon will explode while the other remains collapsed. The same principle operates in preemie lungs. Doctors have to try to get the best lung expansion they can, but if they use too much pressure, they can overinflate and damage some lung sacs while others remain uninflated.

Natural surfactant can be collected from cow lungs, but many babies have an adverse reaction to it. The solution to the surfactant problem came in the late 1980s, when artificial surfactant was developed and approved for use in patients. The artificial surfactant performs the same as the natural substance by keeping the lungs from collapsing and making it easier for them to expand evenly.

The invention of artificial surfactant has made an incredible difference in preemie survival. In the early 1980s, babies born after only twenty-six to twenty-eight weeks of gestation had just a one-in-three chance of surviving—and 90 percent of those that did survive had long-term developmental difficulties. Now the statistics are much better: such early preemies stand an 80 percent chance of surviving, and most will catch up to a regular developmental schedule in a few years. Even more dramatic is the change since Patrick Kennedy died. In 1963, only about 3 percent of the children born as early as he survived. Now 97 percent survive.

The future may yield even more impressive improvements for helping preemies breathe. Doctors are testing how breathing a fluid, called perfluorocarbon, can carry oxygen into babies' lungs and carbon dioxide out. One benefit of using fluid is that it gently opens the lungs without the need for pressure from a mechanical respirator. Some pressure must be used to push air directly into the lungs, even with surfactant. Doctors might also use perfluorocarbon temporarily to carry surfactant into the lungs and help coat them evenly, something that increases surfactant's effectiveness but is difficult to achieve by other methods. Another benefit is that the fluid is unusually good at getting oxygen into the bloodstream, according to Donald Shaeffer, the Philadelphia physician who is spearheading research on perfluorocarbons. Tests indicate that perfluorocarbon can get oxygen into the baby's bloodstream when he is born after eighteen to twenty weeks in the womb. This is about four weeks before the lungs start working well enough to use air, even with surfactant. The use of perfluorocarbons could therefore push back by a month the limits of a fetus' viability.

Physicians are also coming close to gaining approval for improving preemie breathing with a gas that is usually associated with air pollution. Nitric oxide gas, in addition to being a common pollutant, is a critical signal the body uses, in very small quantities, to dilate blood vessels. Tiny amounts of nitric oxide in the lungs can enlarge the blood vessels in the lungs and allow them to absorb more oxygen.

Until recently, breathing problems have been the major killer of premature infants. Now that medical scientists are gaining on that killer, they are discovering other, more subtle, things that help preemies survive and develop.

The Kangaroo Factor

Kangaroos are the ultimate preemie caregivers. Baby kangaroos and other marsupials spend a relatively short time in the womb, a shorter time than any of their mammal cousins. A kangaroo baby, called a joey, will emerge from the womb into the world just four or five weeks after conception. The immature sprite, less than an inch long, uses his relatively well developed forearms to pull himself, unassisted, through his mother's hair and up her belly. The point of this Australian crawl is to reach the pouch, the natural incubator where he can eat and grow for many months more. Once the joey is snuggled in the pouch, he clamps down on his mother's nipple, which expands in his mouth to lock him in place. Warmed by his mother's body and constantly hooked up to the chow line, the joey may grow for up to ten months more before he is ready to venture off on his own. (This is one animal, though, that can return to the womb, or at least the pouch, when the world seems too frightening—until he gets too big.)

Perhaps kangaroos can teach us a few things about what is really important during the last few months of development, both in the womb and on the preemie ward. For instance, is warmth, oxygen, sustenance, and protection from the outside world all that a mother supplies to her little one? Is that all doctors have to provide to help a premature baby develop properly?

For humans, the answer is generally accepted to be no. Human contact—stroking, touching, holding, and rocking—seem to improve babies' health and make them grow faster. No one can give a technical reason why. In fact, this commonsense emotional need for physical caring wasn't always accepted by doctors because it ran counter to the standard medical doctrines. After the earliest days of preemie care, when doctors at the turn of the century saved babies just by keeping them warm, the biggest threat became infection. Although the invention of "miracle drugs" such as penicillin in the 1930s and 1940s helped a little, doctors continued to do everything possible to isolate preterm babies from contact with people. Old photos from the 1950s and 1960s show premature babies in hermetically sealed plastic boxes, attended by masked and gowned doctors who made infrequent contact with them through gloves built into the side of the box. Parents could see the babies, but they couldn't hold or even touch them. At the time, this seemed like a good idea. If infections were such a threat to the baby, his best hope seemed to be to keep him in conditions as sterile as an operating room for the remainder of his stay in the preemie ward. The outside world is rife with germs, the reasoning went, and any stray germ that slipped through to the child might be the one that kills him.

In the 1960s some researchers, including Stanford psychiatrist Herbert Leiderman, started to worry that the increasingly technological and sterile environment of preemie care was robbing parents and children of an important emotional bond. Parents of children in the neonatal intensive care unit reported that when they did get their child home they often felt a little estranged from the baby and unsure of themselves. The preemie ward began opening up to parents when studies demonstrated that the threat of infection didn't demand pristine conditions. Doctors found that as long as visitors washed their hands, infections were no more common than they had been when there was a bacteriological Maginot Line separating baby from adult. Parents who helped to care for their babies in the ward reported that they not only felt more confident in caring for the babies when they got them home, but they were also more able to interpret the babies' desires and calm them when they were upset. In short, parents felt a greater emotional bond with their child, and the child responded better to them. And so the concept of "bonding" was born.

The benefits of touch, though, go beyond the emotional realm. By the mid 1980s, researchers accumulated hard medical evidence that preterm babies actually did better physically when they had regular human contact. Evidence was first found in rats through research by Saul Schanberg of Duke University School of Medicine. He found that baby rats that were not touched by their mothers grew more slowly than those that were, even though they all ate the same amount of food. He also found that the mother's presence was not needed to restore normal growth—if the babies were simply stroked with a wet paintbrush, they resumed rapid growth.

Schanberg and Tiffany Field of the University of

Miami Medical School demonstrated the benefits of touch in human babies. They showed that if parents or care-givers stroked the babies and moved their limbs for just fif-teen minutes daily, the infants gained almost 50 percent more weight every day, matured more quickly, and cut their hospital stays by an average of six days. Other re-searchers found that the benefits of stimulation continued after the babies were sent home with their parents. In one study, researchers tried to simulate some of the physical sensations of the last trimester of pregnancy for preemies. The scientists found that after completing the program, the infants sucked better, had a more regular heartbeat and better breathing, and showed a wider variety of hand movements.

Schanberg speculates that the effects of touch are based in primitive survival tactics shared by all mammals. Be-cause mammals are extremely dependent on their moth-ers for survival, they may be programmed to slow their metabolism to conserve energy when their mothers are not around to touch them.

Such research has compelled many hospitals to emu-late the marsupials and provide what is known as "kan-garoo care," in which a premature infant, naked except for a diaper and cap, is cradled to a parent's chest. The prac-tice originated in developing countries that didn't have the money for advanced neonatal care. Because of the proven physical and emotional benefits to the infant and parent, kangaroo care is now practiced in technologically advanced neonatal intensive care units around the globe.

The X Factors

Even with all the impressive improvements in prenatal care in the last decade, babies are still smaller after spending time in the preemie ward than they would be if they had continued growing in the womb. The babies that do the best in the neonatal intensive care unit—the ones that have no major problems and grow well—typically weigh no more than five pounds by the date they were originally due to be born. It usually takes about three years for them to catch up to other kids in height and weight. So there are obviously some things that help infants during the last trimester in the womb that they don't get in the hospital. The challenge for the future will be to identify those missing factors.

There are already hints. There are likely hormones or other growth factors supplied through the amniotic fluid or placenta. One such factor has already been mentioned: the unknown substance in the amniotic fluid that seems to help the gastrointestinal tract develop. The mother herself probably supplies some important molecular signals that promote development. Scientists from England's Medical Research Council have discovered that premature babies who are given breast milk instead of formula end up with higher IQs by the time they are 8 years old. The scientists assume that the IQ difference may be the result of some factor in the breast milk that fosters brain growth. Breast milk is known to contain hormones and other biologically important molecules that formula doesn't have.

The placenta, that great factory of hormones and other molecules, is one obvious place to look for growth promoters. After all, that organ is part of the baby during his time in the womb. As we saw in Chapter 3, the placenta is specifically created not only to exchange oxygen and waste products with the mother, but also to create the chemical compounds critical for growth. One problem in identifying those factors is that there is still so little known about exactly what the placenta does. "You can see the difficulty if you look at how many placentologists there are on the staff," says David Stevenson. "There are none." And very few placental specialists in the world, he adds.

The key role that growth hormones from the placenta and the mother probably play in fetal development is the reason that medical experts now recommend that doctors give pregnant women steroid hormones immediately if it seems that they will go into labor prematurely. These steroids will dramatically accelerate the maturation of babies' vital organs. Preterm babies whose mothers were given steroids before their birth have a significantly reduced risk of problems with hemorrhage, heartbeat, and breathing. The steroids work so quickly that doctors find benefits when they are administered as little as twenty-four hours before birth. Unfortunately, the National Institutes of Health has found that fewer than 20 percent of those eligible for the treatment receive it, mostly because doctors don't know enough about when it should be used.

Of course, steroids act broadly, and their use has unintended side effects. Doctors hope they will eventually be able to identify and manufacture the body's many individual growth factors. If physicians know enough about these growth factors and how they function in the womb, they may be able to use them like medicines, administering them to the developing baby exactly when they are needed.

The Future for Preemies

The day when doctors know enough about growth factors that they can dab a little factor Y behind the ear at week 32 and inject a milligram of factor Z during week 33 is still a ways off. So are the days when babies will be able to spend most of their development in some kind of artificial womb. But doctors will soon be able to monitor preemie jaundice by analyzing the chemicals in their breath or sweat. They will soon monitor how well tissues are getting oxygen and where preemies are suffering internal bleeding by shining select wavelengths of light through them. By applying a vast span of technologies, doctors have saved more preterm babies and pushed the limits of preemie survival back to about the twenty-second week of gestation.

All of this comes at a price, however. Many of the earliest births result in million-dollar babies: a stay in the neonatal intensive care unit can cost $12,000 and last several months. There is also the emotional price paid in feelings of guilt, torment, and a family's sense of powerlessness as they watch their child struggle week after week. There is the price to the child himself because he is more likely to have physical and intellectual problems throughout his life, and a cost to society if one more of its members is not able to live up to his full potential. Those physician-researchers at the leading edge of neonatal care stress that saving the one-pound babies born sixteen weeks prematurely is dramatic, but the far more important development will be stopping premature births in the first place. Medical scientists will have truly succeeded when they understand the physical and biochemical events of the last trimester and can apply what they know to help the baby stay and grow inside the womb as he prepares for his first matriculation, which comes in due time.

actual size

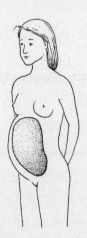

THE NINTH MONTH

(Weeks 35–38 after conception;
weeks 37–40 after LMP)

The baby is finally at his and his mother's physical limits. As a result, his rate of growth slows in the last few weeks of gestation, although he is putting on fat faster than ever. During the last weeks, he is gaining 14 grams (½ ounce) of fat every day, and by his due date over 15 percent of his body weight is fat. The baby has also stored away a great deal of the heat-producing brown fat in certain spots around vital organs. After birth, white fat will help keep heat in and the brown fat will provide immediate warmth.

In the baby's brain, nerve networks are monitoring the brain's own development and that of the rest of the body. Recent research indicates that the baby's brain begins the process of birth when his body and brain are physically ready.

The lanugo and vernix caseosa almost completely disappear in this last month, although a few spots may remain on the back or in folds of the skin. The shed lanugo is swallowed by the baby and accumulates in his bowel (along with other secretions and free-floating cells). This forms a green-black ooze called meconium, which will be the baby's first bowel movement after birth.

By term, most babies are about 50 centimeters (20 inches) long from head to heels, and weigh between 3 and 3.6 kilos (6 lbs. 10 oz. and 7 lbs. 15 oz.). Even curled up, the baby is 36 centimeters (14 inches) long. If he is upside-down, his head is pressing into the mother's pelvis and his rump is pressed up into her rib cage and diaphragm—sending his mother to the bathroom to urinate constantly and causing her heartburn after meals. During these last few weeks, Mom will get some relief with the "lightening," when the baby drops down into the pelvis so his head is fully engaged, and the pressure on the diaphragm is lessened somewhat.

NINE

PARTUM IS SUCH SWEET SORROW

CHEMICALLY AND HORMONALLY, BIRTH CONTRADICTS
everything that has gone on before. Labor is the wild,
rock-and-roll, boogie-woogie, kick-the-dishes-off-the-table-
and-get-down dance after a long conversation and dinner.

For nine months, the body has performed an extraordinary feat in quieting and calming the muscles that
would otherwise expel the fetus. (Left to their own devices, the mother's abdominal muscles would tend to
slowly squeeze out such a foreign body.) Then, at around

thirty-eight weeks, when the fetus is ready to come out, the mother's body violently reverses its former policy and initiates powerful muscle activity. How does the mother's body accomplish this paradoxical process?

The chemical story of how labor begins has been pieced together over the past decades. Although many pieces of the puzzle remain undiscovered, scientists now know enough to sketch the outline of the process, giving them hope that they will be better able to gently help labor proceed at term or effectively hold off preterm birth. In addition, the discoveries so far paint a beautiful picture of a biochemical conversation between mother and child throughout pregnancy. It seems that this conversation proceeds right up to term, and that the fetus has a large say in exactly when labor will begin.

Quiet Time

An old cartoon by Kliban, in two frames, shows a picture of a man standing still over the caption: "The anti-jumping muscles tensed." The other frame shows the man jumping, and underneath is the caption: "The anti-jumping muscles relaxed." Although the cartoon is patently ridiculous as an anatomy lesson, it does illustrate an important principle of how pregnancy is maintained. Sometimes it takes a lot of activity to get nothing to happen.

During pregnancy, the bands of muscles that circle the mother's abdomen are actively quieted by progesterone. The importance of this hormone in maintaining pregnancy is dramatically demonstrated by the controversial abortifacient RU-486, which works primarily by blocking the activity of progesterone. Progesterone also keeps the cervix firm in order to keep it from opening too soon.

But muscles that aren't used atrophy, so progesterone production is shadowed throughout pregnancy by its doppelganger, estrogen. Estrogen, unlike progesterone, promotes the contraction of these abdominal muscles. Throughout pregnancy, the mother keeps the ratio of these hormones tilted toward progesterone, with enough estrogen to promote the mild contractile activity that keeps the abdominal muscles toned and ready for action. There are two kinds of contractions that take place during pregnancy: type A contractions, in which isolated muscles tense individually, and type B contractions, in which many muscles are involved. Type B contractions are also called Braxton-Hicks contractions. Although both types occur throughout pregnancy, some women may not feel them.

During the last few weeks of pregnancy, the production of estrogen slowly starts to increase. This causes a number of important changes. First, estrogen promotes the production of contractile proteins. The hormone also promotes the formation of gap junctions, tunnels between adjacent muscle cells that will carry contraction signals rapidly from one cell to another. This makes it possible for the muscles to tense simultaneously, with no signal from the brain.

Estrogen also prompts cervical ripening, or softening in preparation for the passage of the baby. During most of the pregnancy, the cervix is a hard, thick plug of fibrous tissue about the size of the thumb. Estrogen helps the hormone relaxin bind to the cervical tissue. This action produces enzymes that break down connective tissue in the cervix and relax it, just as enzymes change a ripening peach from a hard, green ball into a soft, juicy fruit. The softening cervix then begins the effacement, or thinning and shortening, that obstetricians measure in the last month of pregnancy.

One critical role of the increased level of estrogen is to make the mother's blood coagulate more easily. This is necessary because many capillaries will be broken as the baby pushes through the birth canal and the placenta pulls away from the uterine wall during labor. To keep blood loss to a minimum, the blood clots more quickly. Interestingly enough, this crucial function is probably the basis of a rare but dangerous side effect of estrogen-rich birth control pills and hormone replacement therapy: both can cause dangerous blood clots.

Finally, and most important for the start of labor, the increase in estrogen triggers the creation of the two final levers of labor: prostaglandin and the receptors for oxytocin.

Oxytocin and Prostaglandin

Both prostaglandin and oxytocin cause strong contractions of the uterus. They are the chemicals that drive hard labor.

Among the two, oxytocin is thought to be most responsible for early labor. This hormone is released from the mother's pituitary, a pea-shaped gland located at the base of the brain. Sometimes doctors accelerate the natural progression of labor by administering Pitocin, an artificial form of oxytocin. In the last days of pregnancy, estrogen prompts a 100- to 200-fold increase in the number of oxytocin receptors in the muscles surrounding the uterus. Receptors are the structures that sit in cell membranes and transmit the message from molecule (oxytocin) into the muscle, making it contract. So an increase in oxytocin receptors can increase muscle contractions without any increase in oxytocin itself. An increase in receptors also makes the muscles over-react to any future increase in oxytocin levels.

That release of extra oxytocin comes as the baby's head begins to push at the cervix under the influence of gravity and light contractions. Nerve fibers in the area of the cervix then send messages to the mother's pituitary to release oxytocin. The burst of oxytocin causes more contractions, which pushes the baby's head harder against the cervix, which leads to more oxytocin release. Squeezing the mother's nipples can also send signals to the pituitary to release oxytocin (the chemical is extremely important for milk release during nursing). Many doctors recommend that women in early labor keep walking and squeeze their nipples, both of which help release oxytocin. Oxytocin released by the fetus, as opposed to that released by the mother, may also be important in early labor.

Prostaglandin is thought to be the workhorse of active labor. Like oxytocin, prostaglandin induces strong contractions in the muscles that circle the uterus. Artificial prostaglandin analogues can also be used to promote the initiation of labor.

Who starts labor, mother or child? Scientific evidence indicates that it's the child who monitors the progress of his own development, and whose brain sends out many of the first signals to begin labor.

The first clues that this is true appeared in the 1960s. Sheep in Idaho were bearing their young long past their due dates. Scientists found that the glands that governed their response to stress were not acting properly. It was determined that the sheep were eating a toxic plant called skunk cabbage that caused deformities in the late-born lambs, particularly in part of the brain called the hypothalamus and in the nearby pituitary.

In the 1970s, New Zealand obstetric researcher Mont Liggins began to study the problem during a sabbatical at the University of California, Davis. There, and later with his colleagues at the National Women's Hospital in Auckland, he found that the lambs were born on time only if their system for governing their responses to stress, called the HPA (hypothalamic-pituitary-adrenal) system, was functioning properly. If fetal stress hormones were not produced, birth would be delayed. If the development of the fetal adrenal glands was accelerated and stress hormones were produced early, birth was premature.

In the early 1990s, Peter Nathanielsz and Thomas McDonald at Cornell University showed that the original signal for birth was emitted by a small area of the fetus's brain in the hypothalamus called the PVN (paraventricular nucleus). This signal prompted the hypothalamus to release its message to the pituitary, which in turn stimulated the release of stress hormones from the fetal adrenal glands.

These hormones start the process of labor when they travel to the placenta, where they promote the production of estrogen and suppress the production of progesterone. The stress hormones also make enzymes that actually change progesterone into estrogen. All this shifts the critical progesterone/estrogen ratio and begins the changes leading up to labor.

The brain, particularly the hypothalamus, is a superb spot for controlling the time when labor begins. Because the brain has connections to all parts of the body, it can monitor the activity and development of all the body's critical components. In all mammals, the hypothalamus itself acts as the primary controller of hunger, the biological clock, body temperature regulation, sexual behavior, the stress response, and the endocrine hormonal system. With such broad responsibilities, this one small part of the brain has a direct line to every important physiological function in the body. The hypothalamus is able to gather together lines of communication from all the body's organizational units and create a forum for consensus; when all systems are "go," the hypothalamus ticks over the first chemical domino that will lead to labor.

If this is what happens in sheep, does it also happen this way in humans? Scientists don't yet know, but there are indications that the basic scheme is the same. Monkeys follow a similar plan, with the fetus's hypothalamus activating stress hormones; only the type of stress hormone and their mode of action differs. Children with certain birth defects that affect the pituitary can be many weeks past due (although if a baby is past due by many days or even over a week, it probably does not mean that there is any defect—many births are past due up to two weeks because of a slightly slower rate of development or a mistake on the due dates).

The other common question this raises is whether extreme stress in the mother can supply enough stress hormone to trigger labor. It seems not. The stress hormones involved do not cross the placental barrier, and the stress hormones seem to need to be present inside the placenta. Stress hormones given to pregnant monkeys do not cause premature birth. Stress in an expectant mother can nevertheless have other detrimental effects on the developing baby (see Chapter 5) and should be avoided for that reason. And although stress hormones are a healthy part of the birth process, extra stress in the mother can slow down the birth and extreme stress in the baby can create difficulties for him as he makes the transition to life outside the uterus.

But how much say does the mother have in when birth occurs? It seems that, as is so often the case in life, the mother plays the role of gatekeeper in the affair, exerting her influence on what time of day birth occurs. In his fascinating book *Life Before Birth and a Time to Be Born*, Peter Nathanielsz points out that animals generally go into labor during what would normally be their sleeping time. If the animals are nocturnal sleepers, they find an isolated spot as darkness falls and go into labor. If monkeys in captivity are kept on a fixed light/dark timetable, they usually go into labor during the early hours of darkness. Humans, too, often go into labor during the early evening hours. In addition, many women at the end of their term often experience a false labor on the nights preceding actual labor. The contractions on those nights grow stronger (and perhaps even painful) in the early evening hours, leading the women to wonder if this is the real thing. However, these contractions don't lead to a dilation of the cervix, and their frequency doesn't increase. It seems that, as the fetus pulls the chemistry of the womb inexorably toward labor, something in the mother's twenty-four-hour clock is opening and closing a window of opportunity, a window of time in which birth is more likely. As throughout pregnancy, mother and child carry on a chemical conversation, deciding, on a subconscious level, that the time is right.

Fission Reaction

Explosions are the result of self-amplifying chain reactions. Each link of the chain amplifies the reaction of the next link. Fission bombs offer a simple example. When a neutron hits an atom of uranium, the neutron breaks up the atom, which releases energy and three neutrons. These three hit three more uranium atoms, each of which release another three neutrons, and so on. Chemical explosions operate on a similar principle.

Obviously, these types of self-amplifying reactions are usually not a good idea for the chemical reactions in our bodies. They respond to excess with more excess. And, in fact, chemical actions in biology almost always have negative feedback. Any action sets in motion an opposite reaction that returns the system to equilibrium. Rising blood sugar prompts the release of insulin, which brings down blood sugar, which cuts down on insulin release. A self-amplifying mechanism in this case would quickly clear the blood of all sugar, leading to coma and death. Not a good idea.

The separation of mother and child is one of the rare cases in biology where a self-amplifying reaction is a good idea, because a crescendo of muscle activity is absolutely necessary to expel the fetus, and because there is a definite end point when the whole process will shut down. All the factors described previously reinforce each other and amplify the effects of the next links in the chain reaction. Labor is an uncontrollable fission reaction.

As mentioned previously, the process begins many days before, when estrogen levels begin to rise and progesterone levels fall (probably as a result of fetal secretion of stress hormones). This causes the cervix to soften and the muscle cells around the womb to gear up for labor. In the days leading up to the time of delivery, the balance of progesterone, estrogen prostaglandins, and oxytocin begins to tip over the critical point as light contractions begin to increase. At some point, the power of progesterone to suppress contractions is overcome by the action of oxytocin and prostaglandin as they stimulate muscle activity. Contractions push the baby against the cervix, which causes oxytocin release from the mother's pituitary, which in turn causes stronger contractions. Progesterone is increasingly manufactured and released. The gap junctions, molecular tunnels between muscle cells, carry contraction signals instantaneously around the abdomen, so that the muscles tense together, without need of the nervous system. Indeed, the labor muscles are operating on a very basic level, beyond the domain of conscious control.

The contractions that start out as much as a half-hour apart slowly increase their frequency and their strength, coming every fifteen minutes, then every ten, every eight, every few minutes. By this time the contractions are very hard and the cervix is widening. When the contraction hits the baby's heart rate slows as his heart works harder against the pressure. The muscles are pushing against the baby with about the same pressure you would feel if you lay on your back and put your hand under your bottom. In other words, the contraction might really hurt for the mother, but for the baby it's just a hard squeeze. The slowing of blood flow is usually no problem either, since fetuses have a special type of hemoglobin that grabs oxygen more strongly and gives it up more slowly than adults, giving them an extra buffer during brief interruptions in the blood supply.

When the cervix comes close to opening the full ten centimeters that signal complete dilation, the baby's head begins to move through into the birth canal, pushing downward and turning ninety degrees, a trick to get the large head through the pubic opening. The amniotic sac has broken by this time, and the contractions and the narrow passage through the birth canal squeeze amniotic fluid from the baby's lungs, preparing them for their first breath. Then, with the mother making a conscious effort to push, the baby crowns and then slips out into the world.

For the newborn, many things happen quickly. Right away, the umbilical cord starts to close down around the blood vessels inside, and usually it is quickly clamped and cut. The combination of the cool, dry air and the oxygen debt that has built up during the baby's passage through the birth canal creates a kind of automatic startle response, and the baby takes in his first breath of air. A little patting or rubbing on the baby's back helps this process along. A good, throaty cry forces open most of the little sacks in the lungs. A good cry can also help warm the baby, because evaporation from his wet body quickly lowers his temperature before he can be swaddled.

Once his lungs are inflated, the baby's heart has to completely reroute his blood supply to bring it through the lungs. Before birth only about 10 percent of the blood

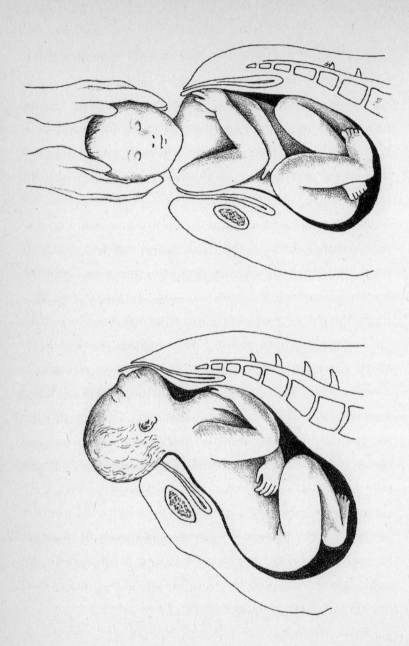

passes through the lungs, the rest passing through a valve in the wall of the heart or through a blood bypass called the ductus arteriosus. When the lungs inflate, blood begins to pass through them, changing the pressure in the heart and immediately closing the valve in the wall of the heart. The ductus arteriosus also begins to close, but doesn't fully shut off blood flow for days.

The Apgar test basically measures how the baby is making the transition from his wet world to dry land. The test (named after Virginia Apgar) is taken at one minute after birth and five minutes after birth. The baby is given a score of 0–2 in each of five categories: heart rate, respiratory effort, color, muscle tone, and reflexes. The first three measure the baby's circulatory state: if the lungs have expanded and breathing is normal, if the blood flow has been rerouted through the lungs. The last two (muscle tone and reflex) measure the responsiveness of the baby's nervous system. A score of 7–10 indicates a healthy baby, although the scores are somewhat subjective and usually change between the one- and five-minute mark.

Once the Apgar scores have risen to the healthy range, the baby is ready for his next transition, ready to put his lips to a nipple and make his first excursion in the dry outerspace of life beyond the womb.

LIFE AFTER BIRTH

A CENTURY OF SCIENCE HAS UNDERMINED THE PHILOSO-
pher William James, who thought that a newborn would
experience sheer chaos as all his senses came into play at
once. "The baby," James wrote in a famous essay in 1890,
"assailed by eyes, ears, nose, skin, and entrails at once,
feels it all as one great blooming, buzzing confusion."
Being born is almost certainly at least a little confusing,
but we now know that many of the senses have long been
at work in the womb, so that the newborn baby can make

at least some sense of the voices, smells, touch, and taste in his new world.

The theme that emerges from our new knowledge of life in the womb is that birth is not so much a beginning or ending as it is a landmark along the way. Many of the things that we think of as part of life after birth—inhaling and exhaling, learning, hearing, tasting—are part of pre-natal life, too. And just as baby's abilities to do these things don't start after birth, the most basic processes of development don't stop at birth. In many ways, prenatal development continues on after birth, outside the womb. For humans, development is extended, the time at which we reach full adulthood delayed in comparison to other animals. Ironically, this developmental delay is an intrin-sic part of what makes us advanced. Many of the ways that we are intelligent and creative as adults come from those elements of infant development that our bodies hold on to long after we leave childhood. And conversely, many of the skills that we most closely associate with adulthood and later childhood—aptitudes in math, lan-guage, mechanics and music—are present in nascent form just months after birth.

But even as the baby is acquiring new intellectual skills, he is struggling with the physical demands of the transition to life outside the womb.

Bugs in the Belly

One of the most immediate trials for the newborn baby is learning to live with the myriad microbes that inhabit the world around us. As pointed out in Chapter 8, disease-fighting immunoglobulin proteins are pulled across the placenta and into the baby's bloodstream while he is still in the womb. The mother's immunological experience and protection continues after birth, as immune proteins in breast milk pass to the baby through his stomach and intestines. There is even some evidence that the mother's lymphocytes, the cells that create immune proteins and carry her immunological memory, can pass into the baby's bloodstream through his young gut. After about six months, the baby's own immune system matures enough to protect him.

Not all microbes pose a threat, however. In fact, we all have an immense number of beneficial bacteria in our intestines, which help us digest food. They are so numerous that over 80 percent of the dry weight of adult feces is dead bacteria. The presence of these good bacteria also protects us against disease-causing microbes. Bacteria set up their environment just the way they like it, creating a certain acidity and putting to good use the resources they have at hand. Harmful bacteria coming into the intestines often have a hard time finding a niche for themselves among the resident bacteria, which far outnumber them. Therefore bothersome microbes aren't able to reproduce and are eventually destroyed by the baby's immune system or the good bacteria. Sometimes harmful bacteria do gain a foothold, or antibiotics, or strange (often spicy) food disrupts the natural ecosystem of bacteria, and the result is diarrhea.

When babies emerge from the womb they are coming from an environment that is virtually sterile, so their immediate task is to get the right bacteria to settle in their intestines. The trick is to get the good bacteria to immigrate before the harmful ones settle in.

Dwayne Savage, a microbiologist at the University of Tennessee at Knoxville, has studied how bacteria colonize the gut after birth. He has found that each animal species has its own mix of resident bacteria in the intestines and its own pattern of establishing it after birth. In humans, beneficial bacteria move in fairly quickly: they start occupying the intestines within the first few days, and within three to four weeks they have established what appear to be the sort of colonies we adults have. Still, it takes longer—six months to a year—for the bacteria to fully form a mature, bacterial ecosystem, Savage says. During that time the baby may be slightly more susceptible to stomach problems.

One of the more interesting immigrants to make the

baby its home is *Streptococcus mutans,* which is not nearly so benign as its intestinal colleagues. *S. mutans* lives in the mouth and causes cavities. The odd thing is that everybody has his or her own variant of *S. mutans,* and most mothers seem to pass on their variety to their children (through kissing, perhaps, or sharing spoons during feedings) during a window of infectivity in the first few years of life. If the transfer is not made, children have fewer cavities. Even stranger is the finding that adopted children seem to have fewer cavities, perhaps because each strain of bacteria does not transfer as well if parent and child are not blood relatives.

Human Thermostat

Even though a great deal of the activity in the last month of life in the womb is spent preparing for the physical challenge of living in the outside world, there is a lot left to do after birth. This is because the abilities that get babies through birth and their first weeks are not the skills they use for survival in the long run. The squirmy, diapered ones seem to be all set once they've made it through the trial of birth and start breathing on their own. But they still have a big transition to make, most of which goes unnoticed by parents. Babies still have to grow into the tasks of warming up and cooling off, learning the cycles of day and night, and mastering the rhythms of feeding and sleeping.

Many of babies' activities—the way they breathe, sleep, and react to cold and heat—are governed by a start-up kit of skills, a set of temporary reflexes that get them over the first physical hurdles after birth. But these reflexes fade away after the first few months and are replaced by responses that are more like those of older children and adults.

The period of transition is a dangerous time. Increasingly, problems with this transition are suspected to play a role in the syndrome that haunts every parent's worst nightmares, the terror that makes them go to the crib in the middle of the night to make sure that, yes, the baby is still breathing, still warm, his heart is still pumping.

Sudden Infant Death Syndrome (SIDS) is responsible for about 2 unexplained deaths in every 1,000 infants. It strikes more often in winter months, and although there are no symptoms common to all cases, many infants that succumb have had a respiratory infection sometime in the previous two weeks. The biggest commonality in SIDS cases, though, is the infants' age. In 95 percent of all cases, SIDS strikes infants who are between two and four months old. This happens to be precisely when critical reflexes that help the baby survive after birth begin to fade away. Control of vital functions such as heating and cooling passes from the primitive brain stem to higher areas of the brain. There, the control of body systems can be integrated and more actively regulated.

One example of this shift is the regulation of body temperature. From birth to seven weeks, infants maintain a constant body temperature. They then enter a stage in which their temperature drops slightly whenever they sleep, day or night. Then they adopt a new temperature pattern, which remains through adulthood. In this stage, the baby's temperature drops only during nighttime sleep. Some babies, scientists have recently found, don't make this transition when they should, and may take as long as twenty weeks to reach an adult pattern of temperature regulation. This gap, from seven to twenty weeks, is exactly the highest-risk time for SIDS. Furthermore, SIDS cases have been more common in babies who are overbundled in the crib or sleep in overheated bedrooms, which adds circumstantial evidence to the theory that temperature regulation is sometimes involved in the deaths.

The control of breathing and heart rate is also transferred to the higher areas of the brain during this time, creating added risk. If the brain mechanisms that are supposed to take on responsibility for these vital functions are underdeveloped or behind schedule, the brain may end up dropping the ball, giving up control in one area before the other is ready to take over. This could help explain why premature babies have ten times greater chance of SIDS than babies born near term: although the preemie infant has been out of the womb for a few months, the areas of the brain that govern reflexive control of vital functions may start to fade out, while the brain regions that are supposed to take over are not developed enough.

The unseen, mostly unnoticed, transfer of critical functions in the brain underlines an important point: of all the organs in the body, the brain plays the leading role in the postscript to prenatal development. Indeed, it is in the brain that the most amazing changes occur.

Moving Ahead

Every mother learns something about the size of a baby's head. She finds out, through books and firsthand experience, that it's the widest part of the baby, and that that bruising little duckpin bowling ball of a head is at the upper limit of what can possibly fit through the pelvis and the birth canal. Even then, the trick is only accomplished because of the baby's soft skull, which allows the head to deform a little so that the baby can make it to the light at the end of the tunnel.

Anthropologists have also spent a lot of time thinking about the relationship between the mother's pelvis and the size of the baby's head. Over the years they have come up with an interesting observation: no other animal has as much brain growth after birth as humans do. Chimpanzees are born with brains that weigh about 7 ounces, and by adulthood their brains have just about doubled in size and weight. Humans, on the other hand, are born with brains that weigh about 14 ounces, which *more* than double in size *in just the first year after birth.* The brain nearly triples its size (to an adult weight of about 45 ounces) by the time the child is six years old. This is why children's heads are so big: their brain is an adult size, but the body takes ten or fifteen years to catch up!

The dramatic increase in brain growth is nature's way of solving a problem: somewhere millions of years back in human evolution, the push for bigger, smarter brains met the immovable impasse of a birth canal and pelvis that just couldn't get much bigger. The solution was to let the gestation period remain at nine months, but allow brain development to continue as if the baby was still in the womb. Donald Johanson, the anthropologist who discovered the famous hominid "Lucy," puts it this way in his book *Ancestors**: "In essence, every human baby is a 'preemie,' born ahead of the delivery date. Gestation actually lasts for 21 months, and human infants are external

*Written with Lenora Johanson and Blake Edgar.

embryos who go through a year of 'prenatal' development outside the womb."

Part of the price of this extended embryonic period is that humans are quite helpless and dependent for some time after birth. Other animals can lift themselves up on wobbly legs and make efforts to fend for themselves within a few moments of being born, because their brains are more complete, more "fully baked," at birth. The survival skills of human newborns seem limited to sucking, screaming, and flailing.

Of course, taking care of a helpless human infant requires great social cooperation and parental care, which in themselves requires more sophisticated brains on the part of adults—so the evolutionary trend toward bigger brains was self-reinforcing. (Some anthropologists think that this cooperative, intensive care of infants also required a high degree of monogamy, which is unusual for primate groups).

During this extended period of development, mothers are supplying more than food and love. Scientists have recently discovered that in the months after birth, mothers who breastfeed maintain a biochemical link with their infants which fosters that brain growth. In 1994, researchers at the Weizmann Institute of Science in Rehovot, Israel, found that when breasts produce milk they also manufacture a peptide hormone that promotes brain development.

This hormone, called GnRH (gonadotropin releasing hormone), is also produced by the placenta—so the GnRH the baby gets from breastfeeding is a continuation of hormone infusion he received before birth. Hormones such as this may be a large part of the reason that breastfed babies seem to score a little higher on IQ tests in later years. The steady discovery of hormones such as GnRH in breast milk continues to provide powerful ammunition for those who advocate breastfeeding. Interestingly, in 1994, other scientists discovered that the act of breastfeeding also changes mothers' brains; scans of mom's brain activity before breastfeeding is started are different after she has breastfed her baby for a couple of weeks.

Little Smarties

Helpless as they are, infants in the first postnatal years of their lives are far from incapable. Though you can't let them out of your sight, and they haven't yet learned that carrot puree shouldn't be pawed on the white linen sofa, infants have powerful capabilities that have long been overlooked. The tiny neural microprocessors are already whirring away in the brain during their first year, giving babies certain skills in math, physics, language, and music. Through careful observation and testing, scientists in recent years have begun to spot those nascent abilities, and shown that even though babies are not communicating their thoughts on these subjects, they are soaking them up and cogitating on them.

Karen Wynn, a psychologist at the University of Arizona, discovered just how early babies start exhibiting an understanding of basic mathematical principles. She demonstrated that infants only five months old understand adding and subtracting of small numbers of objects. To show this, Wynn took advantage of a well-known principle: babies who see something they don't expect will stare at it longer than they would if they had expected it. First Wynn let an infant see a certain number of dolls— say, two. Then she blocked the babies' view of the dolls with a screen and performed one of two tests. Either she let the baby see her putting one more doll behind the screen, or she added another doll surreptitiously. After the screen was taken away the babies saw three dolls. If the baby had watched the other doll go behind the screen, he signaled that he expected to see three by becoming quickly disinterested. If the extra doll had been added in secret, he stared longer, indicating that duplicating dolls were not what he expected.

Wynn did this experiment with different numbers of dolls, and she subtracted dolls from the scene as well as added them. The data all pointed to one conclusion: even though babies could not recognize and manipulate written numbers, they could perceive and manipulate numerical concepts. This research seems to add further evidence to the idea that numerical abilities are innate, somehow built into brain structures that operate independently from other brain functions.

Scientists at Cornell University in Ithaca, New York, use the same principles of baby attention to study another area: babies' understanding of "common-sense" physics. As with math, it seems that babies have some early, built-in knowledge of how things work. Cornell psychologist Elizabeth Spelke showed babies a number of objects behaving "normally" (falling, bouncing, rolling, etc.) or strangely (balls rolling uphill, balls seeming to roll through solid objects, hanging in the air, etc.). Like the babies who could count Wynn's magically duplicating dolls, babies as young as four months who observed Spelke's objects acting strangely stared at them longer than they did at the objects that behaved as we would expect. Her research demonstrates that babies have an automatic understanding of how objects should normally act, and spot unusual physical behavior.

Young babies also seem to have a sense of music appreciation. Scientists at Stanford University found that infants as young as five months old can recognize appropriate rhythms and musical phrasing. Psychologists John

Pinto and Ann Fernald started their experiment by inserting one-second pauses into sections of music by Bach, Mozart, and Bartók. In some sections they inserted the pauses in places where you might expect it, for example where you might take a breath if you were humming the melody. In other sections, they inserted the pauses in a more random manner, so that the sounds of silence stopped the natural flow of musical phrases.

Then the scientists taught babies that they could turn the music on by looking at a red-and-white checkerboard or turn it off by looking away. On average, babies listened longer to the music with the more natural pauses between phrases, showing they had some innate awareness and appreciation for the "right" rhythms. Interestingly enough, though, the babies only chose to listen to the music with appropriately-placed pauses if the very first section they heard had appropriate pauses. If the first section had strangely placed pauses, they seemed to dismiss it and everything after as just so much noise.

Dismissing the noise is something babies seem to do a lot, and this strategy also happens to be an early, and crucial, part of learning language.

Language: Learning to Forget, Forgetting to Learn

Certain languages are torture to learn as a second language, particularly if you want to learn to speak them well. Many Asian languages such as Chinese and Thai are highly tonal: words that sound exactly the same to non-native speakers are, in fact, slightly different tonal variations with quite different meanings. Sometimes this can lead to amusing or embarrassing incidents. After a year in Thailand, one American exchange student loudly bid goodbye in Thai to a friend and told her she was going to ride her bike home. The friend quietly let her know that she had just said she was going to *fart* her bike home. The two verbs sounded nearly identical to the American.

Studies have shown that newborns and babies a couple months old can distinguish between the multiplicity and ever-so-slightly different sounds found in languages around the world, even sounds they've never heard before. In fact, they can tell the difference between all 150 sounds in human linguistics. But by the time they are a year old, infants are no longer able to distinguish between sounds in their own language and slightly different sounds employed in others. This is because their brain lumps the foreign sound in with the closest approximation in their own language.

Language researchers used to think that babies learned

to exclusively recognize the sounds of their own language *after* they began to understand the meanings of words at about ten months of age. For example, it was thought that children might learn the difference between the sounds for *D* and *L* when they realized that "dog" and "log" stood for different things.

But psychologist Patricia K. Kuhl and her colleagues at the University of Washington in Seattle have shown that by six months of age, babies have already started to learn the key sounds, called phonemes, of their own language. Even before they have begun to understand the words that the phonemes make up, they start to form prototypical examples of the phonemes they will need to learn words in their native tongue. The subtle variations of babies' native language will remain recognizable, but the nuances of other languages' pronunciation will start to blur together. This is why it is difficult for adults to learn to speak a foreign language without an accent. Once, they had the ability to distinguish those sounds, but now they've forgotten how.

Use It or Lose It

Just what is going on in the brain on the cellular level during this extended embryonic stage in the first months and years after birth? Scientists in a wide range of fields are discovering that the brain activities in this period have implications for education in our youth, and for our health and vitality as we grow old.

As mentioned in Chapter 5, by the time the baby is born, he has the full complement of trillions of neurons in the brain, and no new cells are being created. The tremendous growth of the brain, then, comes not from new cells, but the growth of new nerve extensions that reach out to connect up existing cells. The logarithmic explosion of new connections that started in the womb continues to accelerate. Recall that the results of a survey of brain connections for the prenatal period by Peter Huttenlocher of the University of Chicago showed that when the fetus is 24 weeks old, the 70,000 cells in a tiny sample of brain tissue contain about 124 million connections. Huttenlocher found 253 million connections in the same sized sample surveyed at birth. By eight months, the number of connections had more than doubled to 578 million in a piece of brain tissue the size of a pinhead.

At the same time that new nerve connections are forming, many are being weakened or broken. This sort of breaking of connections might account for the pruning of sound recognition discussed earlier: babies are born with the wiring to recognize all language sounds, but through the selective weakening and strengthening of different connections, the ability to recognize some of those sounds is lost. After a baby's first birthday, the weeding out and pruning of excess connections overtakes the growth of new ones. Over the next several years the number of connections in Huttenlocher's tissue sample begins to fall, then stabilizes at 350 million by about twelve years of age.

In short, neurons are reaching out to link up with each other just as they did during prenatal development, but after birth they are doing so at a hugely accelerated rate. And, just as in the womb, new connections are being strengthened, weakened, or eliminated, depending on what neural traffic passes through them. The difference is that, after birth, the neurons receive significantly more physical, emotional, and intellectual stimulation from the outside world. Day by day, the baby is creating a model of the world around him within his brain.

The creation of the baby's mental map of his world has an important "use-it-or-lose-it" aspect. Psychologists have long known that there are "critical periods" in intellectual development when children must learn a skill or lose their ability to learn it. For instance, if children aren't exposed to language (as a result of abuse or abandonment) before about age ten, they permanently lose the ability to learn to talk. What seems to happen on the cellular level is that the areas of the brain that are slated to devote themselves to speech set themselves up and wait for the right form of stimulation—spoken language—to come along. If it doesn't, those neurons eventually give up and devote themselves to other tasks. The same thing happens in the visual system. If cataracts or other eye problems block vision from birth until age two, some visual areas of the brain don't complete their development, and they take on other jobs. After that, no matter how much stimulation the eyes get, those parts of the eye that are clouded will never be able to connect up with the brain areas that they were supposed to. The person will always have impaired vision.

This holds true for many areas of the brain and many other skills. There are certain periods of development when neurons have the potential to become sensitive to tactile, visual, aural, lingual, and emotional stimulation; once the chance slips away, it is gone forever.

Research on how the brain develops is already changing people's perceptions of infant life and altering how they bring up children. Where nurseries were once adorned with the purest white decorations, people now try to supply interesting and colorful wall hangings and toys. Parents are trying to give their children varied sights and sounds to foster brain development. But this research also has broader ramifications that reach into our adult lives and old age.

Forever Young

The saying, "You can't teach an old dog new tricks," while not completely true, captures an important point of development, one that applies to most animal species, including humans. Youth is always inchoate, unformed, and full of potential. Young animals and children spend much of their time playing and exploring. They adapt and learn easily. Adults, on the other hand, are more focused, more purpose-built. Adults are usually more successful at learned skills, but adults also become more fixed and less adaptable as they get older. We old fogies have learned how to play the game, how to ignore the extraneous and get the job done, but in the process we often shut out the play and exploration that makes true creativity possible.

The power of this concept is that it is mirrored at a cellular level. In the earliest embryos, each cell can become any kind of tissue—blood, liver, brain, heart. As embryos grow, cells get locked into certain jobs and become specialized. (When cells do revert to their early state and lose their specialization, the result is usually cancer.) Once they are formed in the embryo, most tissues remain the same for ever after. The skin grows and regenerates itself to compensate for normal wear and tear, but it is unchanged in complexity and structure between the time a baby is born and fifty years later. The heart gets larger, but remains qualitatively the same from birth until it starts failing in old age.

But the brain is a special case. It continues to make changes in character and complexity after birth. In fact, even though the major wiring of the brain is finished by the end of childhood, the shaping of brain circuits doesn't stop there. The resculpting and rewiring happens all the time, all your life. Neurons continue to reach out to each other and connect up. Existing connections are reinforced or weakened. Every time you learn something or commit an event to memory, you are making a physical change in the brain, a change in the brain's chemistry and structure. After reading this book, you will have a different brain than before you picked it up.

The more complex the thing to be learned, the more changes there are to be made in the brain. This can also help us understand why habits are so hard to break, in order to change a behavior, you have to learn a new way of being and physically change a set of brain circuits that are interlocked and strongly reinforced.

What's more, the brain changes involved in learning and memory use many of the tools employed in early development. For the brain, development is an ongoing process, a means in itself rather than just a means to an end. In a sense, the brain is the body's forever young organ, the part of the body made to stay plastic and adapt to new circumstance. Long after the rest of the body has stopped growing and developing, the brain is constructing new networks and connections. Every time something is learned, every time the brain creates a space for a new mental picture, it is an act of development.

Just as in early development, the "use-it-or-lose-it" principle continues to apply. When people keep learning new things, keep exercising their minds they literally continue to keep their brains fit and more open to further learning.

Recently, researchers showed that college graduates who stayed mentally active late in life have about 40 percent more connections between their nerve cells than people who didn't finish high school. Education in itself isn't enough, though. College graduates who didn't stay mentally fit did not have nearly as many neural connections. Other researchers have found that people who exercise their brains into old age are happier, and they may be resistant to neurodegenerative disorders such as Alzheimer's disease.

Souvenirs

What do we bring away from our time in the womb? Some people believe we have memories of life in the womb, and they spend time in hypnosis or therapy trying to retrieve them. But that is a quixotic task. The brain structures that let us remember discrete events don't mature until about two or three years of age. Memories of events in the womb are simply not there to be retrieved. So do we have nothing left from our prenatal sojourn besides a dimple and scar where the umbilical cord was once attached? Have we torn up all the photos from that trip, trashed all the mental videos?

The answer is that, while we don't have concrete memories, the memories we have are bred in the bone, they live on in the way we look and think and learn. The infant lives on in all of us. So many of our adult traits are examples of what anthropologists call "neotony," the carrying through of childhood traits into adulthood. Our high forehead and round face are features common to both human and Neanderthal babies, but are so different than the low brow and primitive appearance of our hominid ancestors in adulthood. Our playfulness and creativity as adults is the source of much of our technology and culture, but in most animal species that playfulness is restricted to the young.

At the cellular level, the brain continues its formation and reformation into adulthood, displaying a plasticity and adaptability that are hallmarks of a developing nervous system. As a species we are special for the long delay between birth and adulthood. We stretch out the processes of development and stay childish for 18 years or so (and more if college and graduate school are included), far longer than any other animal species. And even beyond those years, we stay adaptable, able to learn new skills and form new, complex emotional bonds.

Even though we don't have memories of any particular time in the womb, we carry that time with us all our lives. The elements of prenatal life are so much a part of us as adults that they hardly seem remarkable. They can be found in the calming sound of a heartbeat or the relaxing quality of a warm bath. They live on in the changing brain, in every act of learning or creativity. They visit us every night in our dreams. And as we learn more about prenatal life we can know more about the qualities that we adults still keep from life's maiden voyage. We can find, in our dreams and thoughts and feelings, insight into the souvenirs we picked up on the journey to ourselves.

Index

sensory organs of, 200–201
and stress, 154–55
in transition period, 262–63
breast milk, 235, 258, 265–66
breathing, 215–17, 225–29, 253,
262

CAH (congenital adrenal
hyperplasia), 179–82
calendar vs. lunar months, 7–9
calories, 219
CAMs (cell-adhesion molecules),
93
cancer, 70, 275
cavities, dental, 260
CCK (cholecystokinin), 50, 51
cells:
brain, 144, 146, 148
communication of, 92–93, 148,
150–51, 272
cortical, 146
cumulus, 33
destruction of, 99–100
division of, 21, 22–23, 58–59,
98, 126
dormant genes in, 70
embryo from, 79
of embryonic tissues, 55
folding sheets of, 82–84, 91, 143
germ, 14, 35, 166
instruction of, 86, 91–93,
96–98, 100–102
mergers of, 22
migration of, 86
natural killer, 68
neural, 106, 137, 142–44,
148–49, 150–54, 272–74,
276–77
non-sex, 26–27
position of, 96
reproductive, 26
sex, 14

skin, 143
slime mold, 25–26
specialization of, 100–101,
275–76
stem, 101
support, 79
suppressor, 68–69
T-, 64
white blood, of father, 69–70
cerebral hemispheres, 144, 146
cervix:
dilation of, 253
and estrogen/progesterone
ratio, 251
and oxytocin, 246
ripening of, 244
widening of, 252, 253
chemotherapy, 101
chromosomes, 112
and gender, 164–66, 169–70
cities, 79–81, 91, 99
cleft lip, cleft palate, 90
clitoris, 74, 169, 170
cloning, 23–24
colostrum, 191
computers, self-instructing,
204–6
conception:
and baby's true age, 8–9
moment of, 8
sex and, 27–30
contractions:
estrogen and, 243–45
false, 250
oxytocin in, 245–46, 252
and progesterone, 252
prostaglandin in, 245–46
corona radiata, 32, 33
corpus callosum, 150
corpus luteum, 62
cortex, 146, 149
visual, 205